TEXAS TEST PREP
Practice Test Book
STAAR Reading
Grade 3

© 2014 by Test Master Press Texas

All rights reserved. No part of this book may be reproduced or transmitted in any form or by any means, electronic, mechanical, photocopying, recording, or otherwise without prior written permission.

ISBN 978-1500581442

Practice Test Book, STAAR Reading, Grade 3

CONTENTS

Section 1: Reading Mini-Tests   **4**
    Mini-Test 1: Literary Text   5
    Mini-Test 2: Informational Text   11
    Mini-Test 3: Literary Text   16
    Mini-Test 4: Informational Text   21
    Mini-Test 5: Literary Text   26
    Mini-Test 6: Informational Text   32

Section 2: Vocabulary Quizzes   **38**
    Quiz 1: Use Context to Determine Word Meaning   39
    Quiz 2: Understand and Use Synonyms   42
    Quiz 3: Understand and Use Antonyms   44
    Quiz 4: Use Homographs and Homophones   46
    Quiz 5: Understand and Use Prefixes   48
    Quiz 6: Understand and Use Suffixes   50

Section 3: STAAR Reading Practice Test 1   **52**
    Practice Test 1: Session 1   53
    Practice Test 1: Session 2   65

Section 4: STAAR Reading Practice Test 2   **77**
    Practice Test 2: Session 1   78
    Practice Test 2: Session 2   92

Answer Key   **105**
    Section 1: Reading Mini-Tests   106
    Section 2: Vocabulary Quizzes   109
    Section 3: STAAR Reading Practice Test 1   111
    Section 4: STAAR Reading Practice Test 2   113

Multiple Choice Answer Sheets   **115**
    Section 1: Reading Mini-Tests   115
    Section 2: Vocabulary Quizzes   116
    Section 3: STAAR Reading Practice Test 1   117
    Section 4: STAAR Reading Practice Test 2   118

Section 1: Reading Mini-Tests

INTRODUCTION TO THE READING MINI-TESTS
For Parents, Teachers, and Tutors

How Reading is Assessed by the State of Texas

The STAAR Reading test assesses reading skills by having students read passages and answer questions about the passages. On the STAAR Reading test, students read 5 or 6 passages and answer a total of 48 multiple-choice questions. The test includes both literary and informational texts.

About the Reading Mini-Tests

This section of the practice test book contains passages and question sets similar to those on the STAAR Reading tests. However, students can take mini-tests instead of taking a complete practice test. Each mini-test has one literary or informational passage for students to read. Students then answer 10 multiple-choice questions about the passage.

This section of the book is an effective way for students to build up to taking the full-length test. Students can focus on one passage and a small set of questions at a time. This will build confidence and help students become familiar with answering test questions. Students will gradually develop the skills they need to complete the full-length practice tests in Section 3 and Section 4 of this book.

Reading Skills

The STAAR Reading test assesses a specific set of skills. These skills are described in the TEKS, or Texas Essential Knowledge and Skills. The full answer key at the end of the book identifies the specific skill that each question is testing.

STAAR READING

Mini-Test 1

Literary Text

Instructions

This set has one passage for you to read. Read the passage and answer the questions that follow it.

Choose the best answer to each question. Then fill in the circle for the best answer.

The Top of the Tower

Toby had a fear of heights. He had carried it with him since he was an infant. As a teenager, his fear had only become worse. He talked to his father about it one day.

"I have had enough Dad," he said. "I would love to go rock climbing with my friends. But every time I get too high, I feel sick."

His dad paused as he thought about his son's problem.

"Well Toby," he said quietly, "I can help you. But you will need to face your fear. Are you ready?"

Toby was quiet for a moment.

"I am ready!" he replied bravely.

Toby's father picked up the keys and walked toward the front door.

"We're going into the city!" his father said.

Toby knew what was coming. Toby lived in Paris, France. Located in the heart of Paris, was one of the world's tallest landmarks. It was the Eiffel Tower. Toby knew that visitors were allowed to climb to the very top. The view overlooked the entire city. Nothing was said between the pair as they drove into the city.

They had arrived at the Eiffel Tower when Toby looked up at it and gasped. His stomach turned over.

"I'm not sure if I can do this," he said nervously.

Toby's father sensed his son's worries.

"Don't worry," he said. "I will be with you every step of the way. This is the day that you beat your fears."

Toby stared up at the giant tower. He took a deep breath as they stepped through the entrance. As his father held his hand, they made their way, step by step, towards the top of the building. Once they reached the top, Toby stepped out from the shadows and onto the ledge.

"Wow, Dad!" he said excitedly as he looked over Paris. The city looked so beautiful from the tower that his fear began to fade. He kept his hand firmly on the tower's metal railing just in case. It felt strong and steady. He still felt a small knot of fear in his stomach, but he told himself that he was fine. Just like the tower, he felt strong and steady.

"I told you there was nothing to worry about," his father said.

1. What does the phrase "heart of" mean in the sentence below?

   Located in the heart of Paris, was one of the world's tallest landmarks.

   Ⓐ Streets of
   Ⓑ Edge of
   Ⓒ Center of
   Ⓓ City of

2. Read this sentence from the passage.

   Nothing was said between the pair as they drove into the city.

   Why was Toby most likely quiet?
   Ⓐ He was fighting with his father.
   Ⓑ He was feeling scared.
   Ⓒ He was excited.
   Ⓓ He was having a nap.

3. Based on the second paragraph, what is the main reason Toby wants to change?
   Ⓐ He does not like being teased.
   Ⓑ He wants to make his father proud.
   Ⓒ He is scared that things will get worse.
   Ⓓ He is tired of missing out on doing things.

4 Which words spoken by the father best show that he is understanding and supportive?

- Ⓐ "But you will need to face your fear."
- Ⓑ "We're going into the city!"
- Ⓒ "I will be with you every step of the way."
- Ⓓ "I told you there was nothing to worry about."

5 Read this sentence from the passage.

> **As his father held his hand, they made their way, step by step, towards the top of the building.**

What do the words "step by step" suggest?

- Ⓐ They moved quite slowly.
- Ⓑ They walked a long way.
- Ⓒ They raced each other.
- Ⓓ They made a lot of noise.

6 In the sentence below, what does the word <u>beat</u> mean?

> **This is the day that you beat your fears.**

- Ⓐ Hit
- Ⓑ Blend
- Ⓒ Rhythm
- Ⓓ Defeat

7 The main theme of the passage is about —

Ⓐ taking chances

Ⓑ overcoming fears

Ⓒ making friends

Ⓓ asking for help

8 In the second last paragraph, Toby is described as feeling "strong and steady." The word steady probably means that he feels —

Ⓐ scared

Ⓑ sick

Ⓒ calm

Ⓓ joyful

9 Which word best describes Toby?

Ⓐ Friendly

Ⓑ Funny

Ⓒ Brave

Ⓓ Shy

10 What do the photographs mainly help readers understand?

Ⓐ How scared Toby feels

Ⓑ How beautiful the city of Paris is

Ⓒ How strong the Eiffel Tower is

Ⓓ How high up Toby goes

STAAR READING

Mini-Test 2

Informational Text

Instructions

This set has one passage for you to read. Read the passage and answer the questions that follow it.

Choose the best answer to each question. Then fill in the circle for the best answer.

Rice Crispy Cakes

Rice crispy cakes are popular treats for children. Everybody loves how crunchy they are. The rice crispy and chocolate flavor is always a hit. And they are a perfect treat for sharing with friends. They are quick and easy to make too.

You only need a few simple things to make them. You will need some crispy rice cereal, butter, and a block of milk chocolate. You will also require a small bowl, a medium saucepan, a large saucepan, a baking tray, and patty cake holders.

What to Do

1. Start by pouring the crispy rice cereal into the small bowl.

2. Add 3 to 4 tablespoons of butter. It is a good idea to soften the butter first. Mix everything together with your hands. Just make sure you clean your hands first! You don't want to get dirt or germs through the mix.

3. You should now be able to fill the patty cake holders. Put a clump of the rice cereal mixture into each holder.

4. Next, you need to melt your block of chocolate. Fill a medium saucepan with water. Chop up about 2 ounces of chocolate. Place it in a small saucepan. Place the small saucepan in the medium saucepan. This will allow the hot water to gradually melt the bar of chocolate. Be careful you don't get water in with the chocolate. It will make the chocolate go hard and grainy. When your chocolate has turned to a thick liquid, it is ready to add to your crispy rice mixture.

5. Let the chocolate cool just enough so it does not burn you. Carefully pour a small amount of melted chocolate onto each ball of crispy rice. Make sure that each rice crispy cake is covered.

6. Arrange each crispy cake on the baking tray and place in the oven.

7. Bake them at 350 degrees for about 30 minutes.

8. When they're done baking, take them out of the oven and allow them to cool.

That's it! Your delicious treats are ready to enjoy or share!

1 In the sentence below, what does the word <u>gradually</u> most likely mean?

> **This will allow the hot water to gradually melt the bar of chocolate.**

- Ⓐ Nicely
- Ⓑ Slowly
- Ⓒ Firmly
- Ⓓ Quickly

2 Read these sentences from the passage.

> **You will need some crispy rice cereal, butter, and a block of milk chocolate. You will also require a small bowl, a medium saucepan, a large saucepan, a baking tray, and patty cake holders.**

What would the author be best to use to give this information more clearly?

- Ⓐ Map
- Ⓑ List
- Ⓒ Diagram
- Ⓓ Timeline

3 What is probably the main purpose of softening the butter?
- Ⓐ To make it easier to mix with the cereal
- Ⓑ To help the chocolate melt
- Ⓒ To make the rice crispy cake cook quicker
- Ⓓ To make it easier to measure out

4   What is the main purpose of the passage?
    Ⓐ   To teach readers how to do something
    Ⓑ   To entertain readers with a story
    Ⓒ   To inform readers about crispy rice cereal
    Ⓓ   To compare different types of sweets

5   In Step 3, what does the word <u>clump</u> show?
    Ⓐ   Only a small amount of mixture should be used.
    Ⓑ   The mixture does not have to be a perfect shape.
    Ⓒ   The mixture is made of rice crispy cereal.
    Ⓓ   The mixture should be a smooth round ball.

6   In which step are the patty cake holders first needed?
    Ⓐ   Step 1
    Ⓑ   Step 2
    Ⓒ   Step 3
    Ⓓ   Step 4

7   Which of these would most help the reader make the rice crispy cakes?
    Ⓐ   A picture of a box of cereal
    Ⓑ   A list of different types of cereals
    Ⓒ   A photograph of a rice crispy cake
    Ⓓ   A timeline of the events

Practice Test Book, STAAR Reading, Grade 3

8 Which step does the photograph most help the reader complete?

Ⓐ Step 3

Ⓑ Step 4

Ⓒ Step 5

Ⓓ Step 6

9 According to the passage, what would be the effect of getting water into the melting chocolate?

Ⓐ The chocolate would go hard and grainy.

Ⓑ The chocolate would splash everywhere.

Ⓒ The chocolate would become too runny.

Ⓓ The chocolate would burn and taste bad.

10 Which reason best completes the chart below?

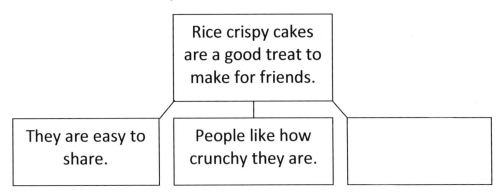

Ⓐ You have to be careful when making them.

Ⓑ You only need a few things to make them.

Ⓒ They take 30 minutes to cook.

Ⓓ The rice crispy and chocolate flavor is a hit.

STAAR READING

Mini-Test 3

Literary Text

Instructions

This set has one passage for you to read. Read the passage and answer the questions that follow it.

Choose the best answer to each question. Then fill in the circle for the best answer.

Little Things
by Ebenezer Cobham Brewer

Little drops of water,
Little grains of sand,
Make the mighty ocean
And the pleasant land.

Thus the little minutes,
Humble though they be,
Make the mighty ages
Of eternity.

This canyon in Arizona is a popular place for tourists and adventure-seekers. People love to admire the lovely view, take photographs, or raft along the Colorado River. It took millions of years for the canyon to form. As water flowed over the land, it wore away the rock little by little. Today, the result is a canyon that is thousands of feet deep.

Practice Test Book, STAAR Reading, Grade 3

1 In the lines below, what does the word <u>eternity</u> most likely mean?

**Make the mighty ages
Of eternity.**

Ⓐ Time
Ⓑ Forever
Ⓒ Earth
Ⓓ Everything

2 Read this line from the poem.

Make the mighty ocean

The word <u>mighty</u> suggests that the ocean is —

Ⓐ strange
Ⓑ scary
Ⓒ powerful
Ⓓ small

3 How many stanzas does the poem have?

Ⓐ 2
Ⓑ 3
Ⓒ 4
Ⓓ 8

4   Which literary technique does the author use in the line below?

   Make the mighty ages

   Ⓐ   Alliteration
   Ⓑ   Simile
   Ⓒ   Metaphor
   Ⓓ   Flashback

5   What is the rhyme pattern of each stanza of the poem?
   Ⓐ   All the lines rhyme with each other.
   Ⓑ   There are two pairs of rhyming lines.
   Ⓒ   The second and fourth lines rhyme.
   Ⓓ   None of the lines rhyme.

6   What are the lines below mainly about?

   **Thus the little minutes,
   Humble though they be,
   Make the mighty ages
   Of eternity.**

   Ⓐ   Nature
   Ⓑ   Earth
   Ⓒ   Time
   Ⓓ   Sleep

7 What is the main idea of the poem?

- Ⓐ Little things can form great things.
- Ⓑ Everything is always changing.
- Ⓒ Life could not survive without water.
- Ⓓ Time can go fast or slow.

8 Which word below is repeated in the poem?

- Ⓐ drops
- Ⓑ mighty
- Ⓒ water
- Ⓓ minutes

9 The canyon is described as deep. Which word means the opposite of <u>deep</u>?

- Ⓐ Shallow
- Ⓑ Simple
- Ⓒ Short
- Ⓓ Small

10 Which idea from the caption of the photograph best relates to the main idea of the poem?

- Ⓐ The canyon is in Arizona.
- Ⓑ The canyon is popular with tourists.
- Ⓒ The canyon offers a lovely view.
- Ⓓ The canyon took millions of years to form.

STAAR READING

Mini-Test 4

Informational Text

Instructions

This set has one passage for you to read. Read the passage and answer the questions that follow it.

Choose the best answer to each question. Then fill in the circle for the best answer.

Roger Federer

Roger Federer is a famous tennis player. He was born in Switzerland in 1981. Some people believe that he is the best tennis player ever. He became the world number one in 2005. He kept this rank for 237 weeks in a row. That is a record! He won 16 Grand Slam titles. That is also a record!

Roger plays well on clay, grass, and hard courts. However, he plays best on grass courts.

Wimbledon is a tennis contest held in Great Britain. Roger has won it six times. In 2008, he tried to win it for the sixth time in a row. He made the final. He was defeated by Spanish player Rafael Nadal. It was a close match. It was tough on both players. It was also great to watch. Some people say that it was the best tennis match ever played. This match also started a long row between the two players.

In 2009, Nadal was having knee problems. He was not well enough to compete in Wimbledon. Federer won that year. In 2010, Nadal beat Roger in the Wimbledon final. The two have competed in eight Grand Slam finals together. Nadal has won six of these.

© Derek Holtham

In 2010, Roger lost his number one ranking. Nadal became world number one. At the start of 2011, Roger was ranked third in the world. He may come back and become number one again. To do this, he will need to beat Nadal.

> While Federer is known for being best on grass courts, Nadal is known for being best on clay courts. He has even been nicknamed "The King of Clay." However, this doesn't mean he isn't great on other types of surfaces as well. He has won Grand Slam titles on hard court, grass, and clay.

1 Read this sentence from the passage.

> **This match also started a long row between the two players.**

As it is used in the sentence, which word means about the same as row?

- Ⓐ Line
- Ⓑ Paddle
- Ⓒ Fight
- Ⓓ Noise

2 In paragraph 3, what does the word defeated mean?

- Ⓐ Beaten
- Ⓑ Watched
- Ⓒ Surprised
- Ⓓ Hurt

3 Where was Roger Federer born?

- Ⓐ Great Britain
- Ⓑ Switzerland
- Ⓒ Spain
- Ⓓ United States

4   What is the first paragraph mainly about?
    Ⓐ   Roger Federer's success
    Ⓑ   Roger Federer's family
    Ⓒ   Roger Federer's problems
    Ⓓ   Roger Federer's childhood

5   Which sentence below is best supported by information in the passage?
    Ⓐ   Nadal dislikes playing Roger Federer.
    Ⓑ   Nadal became a better player than Roger Federer.
    Ⓒ   Nadal looked up to Roger Federer when he was young.
    Ⓓ   Nadal plays better on clay than Roger Federer.

6   Which detail best supports your answer to Question 5?
    Ⓐ   Federer and Nadal played in a match that some people say is the best match ever played.
    Ⓑ   Nadal defeated Federer in 6 out of 8 Grand Slam finals.
    Ⓒ   Nadal is best on clay courts, while Federer is best on grass courts.
    Ⓓ   Federer remained as world number one for 237 weeks.

7   Which detail from the passage is a fact?
    Ⓐ   Roger Federer is the best tennis player ever.
    Ⓑ   Roger Federer will become number one again.
    Ⓒ   Roger Federer was number one for 237 weeks in a row.
    Ⓓ   Roger Federer is a great player to watch.

8 Why didn't Nadal compete in Wimbledon in 2009?

    Ⓐ   He was too young.

    Ⓑ   He had knee problems.

    Ⓒ   He wasn't good enough.

    Ⓓ   He had won too many times.

9 How did Roger most likely feel when he lost the 2008 Wimbledon final?

    Ⓐ   Calm

    Ⓑ   Upset

    Ⓒ   Proud

    Ⓓ   Scared

10 Read this sentence from the passage.

It was a close match.

In which sentence does the word close mean the same as in the sentence above?

    Ⓐ   Kerry tried to close the door quietly.

    Ⓑ   They had to close off the street for the parade.

    Ⓒ   Joanne and Kendra are close friends.

    Ⓓ   James raced past Jonah and won the close race.

Practice Test Book, STAAR Reading, Grade 3

STAAR READING

Mini-Test 5

Literary Text

Instructions

This set has one passage for you to read. Read the passage and answer the questions that follow it.

Choose the best answer to each question. Then fill in the circle for the best answer.

One Game for Two

Thomas could be quite mean at times. He had a younger brother called Simon and he rarely shared his toys with him.

"You must share Thomas," urged his mother. "One day you will want somebody to share something with you and they won't. Then you will be very upset."

Thomas just laughed his mother's advice off.

"I'll be fine, Mom," he replied. "As long as I have my own toys, I will always be fine."

His mother just shrugged her shoulders.

"Very well," she said. "It seems that you know best."

One day she decided to teach him a lesson. Both boys had been begging for a video game system for over a year. She decided that it was finally time to buy the boys the video game system and a few games.

When Christmas day arrived, both boys were patiently waiting for their presents in front of the fireplace. As Thomas tore into the video game package, his eyes lit up. It was the exact video game system he had wanted for so long.

Simon took longer than Thomas to carefully unwrap his own present. When he did, he was delighted to see three video games. He thanked his mother for not just getting him one great game, but getting him three.

Thomas raced over to check out the games. He saw they were the games he wanted as well and grinned.

"There is just one thing, Simon," Simon's mother said. "You don't have a system to play them on, so you're going to have to ask if you can use your brother's."

Thomas's smile turned quickly into a frown.

"But it's my present," Thomas said gruffly. "I don't want him to use it."

"I think you should be kinder and let your brother use it," his mother suggested.

"Do I have to?" Thomas whined.

"You don't have to," his mother said. "But it would be the right thing to do."

Thomas just shrugged. Then he shook his head.

"No," he said firmly. "I've wanted it for ages and I don't want him to break it."

Simon looked at his brother sadly. He wasn't surprised by his decision, but he was still upset by it.

"Very well," the mother said. "But I hope you realize you won't have much fun with your video game system without any games to play."

Thomas suddenly realized that Simon had games, but he didn't. Simon started to say that Thomas could play his games, but his mother stopped him.

"Since you don't want to share your system with Simon, it wouldn't be fair for you to play his games," the mother continued.

Now Thomas realized that he had a problem. He had the system, Simon had the games, and they needed both to be able to play.

Thomas paused and thought for a moment.

"Okay, I suppose I could share my video game system," he whispered quietly. "That does seem fair."

Simon quickly agreed to share his games and they spent the rest of the day playing a racing game together.

1. Read this sentence from the passage.

   He had a younger brother called Simon and he rarely shared his toys with him.

   Which word means the opposite of rarely?
   - Ⓐ Sometimes
   - Ⓑ Never
   - Ⓒ Often
   - Ⓓ Once

2. Read this sentence from the passage.

   As Thomas tore into the video game package, his eyes lit up.

   The word tore suggests that Thomas opened the package –
   - Ⓐ slowly
   - Ⓑ roughly
   - Ⓒ carefully
   - Ⓓ calmly

3. According to the passage, how is Simon different from Thomas?
   - Ⓐ He is selfish.
   - Ⓑ He is older.
   - Ⓒ He is kinder.
   - Ⓓ He is wiser.

4 Why does Thomas most likely grin when he sees the video games?
- Ⓐ He knows that Simon wanted them.
- Ⓑ He doesn't want to show that he is upset.
- Ⓒ He thinks that he will be able to play them.
- Ⓓ He expects his present to be the same.

5 The main theme of the passage is about –
- Ⓐ getting along with your siblings
- Ⓑ sharing your things with others
- Ⓒ buying good presents
- Ⓓ asking for what you want

6 Which sentence best supports your answer to Question 5?
- Ⓐ *One day you will want somebody to share something with you and they won't.*
- Ⓑ *One day she decided to teach him a lesson.*
- Ⓒ *Both boys had been begging for a video game system for over a year.*
- Ⓓ *I've wanted it for ages and I don't want him to break it.*

7 Which word best describes the mother's plan?
- Ⓐ Mean
- Ⓑ Amusing
- Ⓒ Selfish
- Ⓓ Clever

8 Why does Thomas finally decide to share his present with Simon?
- Ⓐ Thomas sees that he is upsetting his mother.
- Ⓑ Thomas realizes that not sharing only hurts himself.
- Ⓒ Thomas begins to feel sorry for Simon.
- Ⓓ Thomas decides he will take the present himself later.

9 Read this sentence from the passage.

> **As Thomas tore into the video game package, his eyes lit up.**

What does the phrase "his eyes lit up" show about Thomas?
- Ⓐ He is pleased and excited.
- Ⓑ He is jealous and annoyed.
- Ⓒ He is interested and curious.
- Ⓓ He is puzzled and confused.

10 Which words spoken by Thomas show that he has changed?
- Ⓐ "I'll be fine, Mom," he replied. "As long as I have my own toys, I will always be fine."
- Ⓑ "But it's my present," Thomas said gruffly. "I don't want him to use it."
- Ⓒ "No," he said firmly. "I've wanted it for ages and I don't want him to break it."
- Ⓓ "Okay, I suppose I could share my video game system," he whispered quietly. "That does seem fair."

STAAR READING

Mini-Test 6

Informational Text

Instructions

This set has two short passages for you to read. Read the passages and answer the questions that follow them.

Choose the best answer to each question. Then fill in the circle for the best answer.

Abraham Lincoln

Abraham Lincoln was the 16th President of the United States. He was born in 1809. He died on April 15, 1865. Lincoln served the United States as President for just short of five years. He is remembered for his strong leadership skills. He led the nation through several conflicts, including the American Civil War.

Abraham Lincoln was born into a poor family. He was mostly self-educated. He worked as a country lawyer. During this period of his life, he also started a family. He raised four children.

His career in politics began at the state level. He was fiercely against slavery. He fought it through national debates. He gave public speeches about the issue. He wrote letters to persuade others to agree with him. His strong opinion won him the support of many. He was then elected president in 1860.

In April 1861, the American Civil War began. Lincoln planned to defeat the South. He wanted to reunify the nation. He oversaw the war effort very closely. He skillfully prevented British support for the South in late 1861. He took control of the civil conflict during the next two years. In 1863, he issued an order that ended slavery. Over 3 million slaves were freed. The war came to an end in 1865. Lincoln achieved his goal of uniting the nation.

Abraham Lincoln was shot and killed just six days after the end of the war. It was a sad end for a man who achieved so much. Abraham Lincoln is thought of by many as the greatest president of all time.

Amelia Earhart

Born in 1897, Amelia Earhart is an American aviation pioneer. She was the first woman to fly solo across the Atlantic Ocean. At that time, it was rare for females to be pilots, let alone be record-breaking pilots! In fact, Earhart was only the 16th woman to be given a pilot's license. She had to fight to achieve her dream of becoming a pilot, and was always having to prove herself to those who thought that women could not handle flying. Earhart set many other aviation records during her life, and also wrote about her experiences. She became a celebrity in the United States, and appeared in many advertisements.

The Purdue University funded an ill-fated flight of the globe in 1937. Sadly, Amelia Earhart and her navigator disappeared over the central Pacific Ocean. To this day, it is unknown what actually happened. Some researchers believe that the plane crashed into the ocean and sank. Another theory is that Amelia landed at an uninhabited island called Gardner Island. There have been many other theories, but none have yet to be proven. It may never be known what happened to Amelia Earhart. However, she can still always be remembered as a great pilot who achieved many incredible things.

Directions: Use "Abraham Lincoln" to answer the following questions.

1. As it is used in the sentence, what does the word <u>fiercely</u> mean?

    He was fiercely against slavery.

    Ⓐ   Usually
    Ⓑ   Quickly
    Ⓒ   Strongly
    Ⓓ   Strangely

2. Read this sentence from the passage.

    He wanted to reunify the nation.

    If the word <u>unify</u> means "to bring together," what does the word <u>reunify</u> mean?

    Ⓐ   To bring together more
    Ⓑ   To bring back together
    Ⓒ   To stop bringing together
    Ⓓ   To bring together before

3. In which year did Abraham Lincoln become president?
    Ⓐ   1860
    Ⓑ   1861
    Ⓒ   1863
    Ⓓ   1865

4   Which paragraph has the main purpose of describing Abraham Lincoln's achievements during the war?

Ⓐ   Paragraph 1

Ⓑ   Paragraph 2

Ⓒ   Paragraph 4

Ⓓ   Paragraph 5

5   In which sentence from the passage does the author give a personal opinion about Lincoln?

Ⓐ   *Abraham Lincoln was the 16th President of the United States.*

Ⓑ   *In 1863, he issued an order that ended slavery.*

Ⓒ   *Abraham Lincoln was shot and killed just six days after the end of the war.*

Ⓓ   *It was a sad end for a man who achieved so much.*

6   Which detail about Abraham Lincoln is least important to understanding why he is considered by some as the greatest president of all time?

Ⓐ   He achieved his goal of unifying the nation.

Ⓑ   He fought to end slavery.

Ⓒ   He was born into a poor family.

Ⓓ   He led America through the Civil War.

Directions: Use "Amelia Earhart" to answer the following questions.

7 Why did Amelia Earhart have to fight hard to achieve her dream?
   - Ⓐ   Flying was quite new and people feared it was unsafe.
   - Ⓑ   People worried that she would have an accident.
   - Ⓒ   She was more interested in being famous than training.
   - Ⓓ   Many people did not think that women could be pilots at the time.

8 What does the word <u>ill-fated</u> suggest about the 1937 flight of the globe?
   - Ⓐ   It cost too much.
   - Ⓑ   It ended badly.
   - Ⓒ   It was poorly planned.
   - Ⓓ   It did not take place.

9 Amelia Earhart was the first woman to fly solo across which ocean?
   - Ⓐ   Atlantic Ocean
   - Ⓑ   Pacific Ocean
   - Ⓒ   Arctic Ocean
   - Ⓓ   Indian Ocean

10 Which sentence best supports the idea that Earhart gained recognition for her achievements?
   - Ⓐ   *In fact, Earhart was only the 16th woman to be given a pilot's license.*
   - Ⓑ   *She became a celebrity in the United States, and appeared in many advertisements.*
   - Ⓒ   *Sadly, Amelia Earhart and her navigator disappeared over the central Pacific Ocean.*
   - Ⓓ   *It may never be known what happened to Amelia Earhart.*

Section 2: Vocabulary Quizzes

INTRODUCTION TO THE VOCABULARY QUIZZES
For Parents, Teachers, and Tutors

How Vocabulary is Assessed by the State of Texas

The STAAR Reading test includes multiple-choice questions that assess vocabulary skills. These questions follow each passage and are mixed in with the reading comprehension questions.

These questions require students to complete the following tasks:
- use context to determine word meanings and distinguish among multiple meaning words
- identify and use synonyms (words that have the same meaning)
- identify and use antonyms (words that have opposite meanings)
- identify and use homographs (words that are spelled the same but have different meanings)
- identify and use homophones (words that are pronounced the same but have different meanings)
- identify the meaning of prefixes and know how they change the meaning of words
- identify the meaning of suffixes and know how they change the meaning of words

About the Vocabulary Quizzes

This section of the practice test book contains six quizzes. Each quiz tests one vocabulary skill that is covered on the state test.

This section of the book covers all of the vocabulary skills assessed on the STAAR Reading test. The aim of the quizzes is to help ensure that students have all the vocabulary skills that they will need for the STAAR Reading test. If students can master this section of the book, they will be ready to answer the vocabulary questions.

Quiz 1: Use Context to Determine Word Meaning

1. What does the word sparkled mean in the sentence below?

    The bright dress sparkled in the sunlight.

    Ⓐ   Shifted

    Ⓑ   Shone

    Ⓒ   Waved

    Ⓓ   Rested

2. What does the word boast mean in the sentence below?

    Candy does boast about her good grades too much.

    Ⓐ   To chat

    Ⓑ   To brag

    Ⓒ   To study

    Ⓓ   To complain

3. What does the word cart mean in the sentence below?

    James had to cart all the books to the library.

    Ⓐ   A vehicle used to move goods

    Ⓑ   A table with wheels

    Ⓒ   To remove

    Ⓓ   To move or carry

4 What does the word <u>adventure</u> suggest?

The game we played was quite an adventure.

- Ⓐ The game was easy.
- Ⓑ The game lasted a long time.
- Ⓒ The game was exciting.
- Ⓓ The game was played by many people.

5 What does the word <u>astonish</u> mean in the sentence below?

We wanted to astonish the class with our special project.

- Ⓐ Amuse
- Ⓑ Scare
- Ⓒ Confuse
- Ⓓ Amaze

6 What does the word <u>chuckle</u> mean in the sentence below?

My friends and I started to chuckle during the movie.

- Ⓐ Cry
- Ⓑ Laugh
- Ⓒ Choke
- Ⓓ Leave

7 If a chat between two people becomes <u>heated</u>, the people are –

- Ⓐ getting angry
- Ⓑ making each other laugh
- Ⓒ feeling calm
- Ⓓ speaking quietly

8 What does the underlined word mean?

Craig had studied for hours. He felt <u>prepared</u> for the test.

- Ⓐ Excited
- Ⓑ Ready
- Ⓒ Nervous
- Ⓓ Pass

9 Which meaning of the word <u>positive</u> is used in the sentences below?

I always try to be positive when I visit my grandmother. I want to make sure I don't make her feel sad.

- Ⓐ Certain or sure
- Ⓑ Upbeat and cheery
- Ⓒ Having good results
- Ⓓ A type of charge

Quiz 2: Understand and Use Synonyms

1. In the sentence below, which word is closest in meaning to <u>whined</u>?

    "I don't feel like going to school," Yani whined.

    Ⓐ   Complained

    Ⓑ   Yelled

    Ⓒ   Whispered

    Ⓓ   Argued

2. Which word means about the same as <u>rush</u>?

    Ⓐ   Wander

    Ⓑ   Walk

    Ⓒ   Push

    Ⓓ   Hurry

3. Which two words have about the same meaning?

    Ⓐ   Spend, save

    Ⓑ   Strong, large

    Ⓒ   Tired, sleepy

    Ⓓ   Sharp, cut

4. Which word is a synonym for <u>loud</u>?

    Ⓐ   Quiet

    Ⓑ   Noisy

    Ⓒ   Busy

    Ⓓ   Sound

5   As it is used below, which word means about the same as weep?

   At the end of the sad book, Alison started to weep.

   Ⓐ   Read
   Ⓑ   Laugh
   Ⓒ   Cry
   Ⓓ   Shout

6   Which word means about the same as perhaps?
   Ⓐ   Always
   Ⓑ   Maybe
   Ⓒ   Certainly
   Ⓓ   Later

7   Which two words have about the same meaning?
   Ⓐ   Polite, rude
   Ⓑ   Last, first
   Ⓒ   Closed, shut
   Ⓓ   Shiny, new

8   Which word is a synonym for trail?
   Ⓐ   Forest
   Ⓑ   Track
   Ⓒ   Cover
   Ⓓ   Ground

Quiz 3: Understand and Use Antonyms

1   As it is used below, which word means the opposite of <u>arrive</u>?

   The visitor was due to arrive at noon.

   Ⓐ   Leave
   Ⓑ   Enter
   Ⓒ   Appear
   Ⓓ   Welcome

2   Which word means the opposite of <u>smooth</u>?
   Ⓐ   Fine
   Ⓑ   Rough
   Ⓒ   Silky
   Ⓓ   Level

3   Which two words have opposite meanings?
   Ⓐ   Brave, tough
   Ⓑ   Cook, burn
   Ⓒ   Correct, wrong
   Ⓓ   Football, baseball

4   Which word is an antonym for <u>early</u>?
   Ⓐ   Close
   Ⓑ   Late
   Ⓒ   Night
   Ⓓ   Near

5   As it is used below, which word means the opposite of common?

   The stamp was too common to be worth anything.

   Ⓐ   Usual
   Ⓑ   Dirty
   Ⓒ   Clean
   Ⓓ   Rare

6   Which word means the opposite of outside?
   Ⓐ   Garden
   Ⓑ   Indoors
   Ⓒ   Beyond
   Ⓓ   Past

7   Which two words have opposite meanings?
   Ⓐ   Whisper, sound
   Ⓑ   Present, gift
   Ⓒ   Pop, snap
   Ⓓ   Tiny, giant

8   Which word is an antonym for bought?
   Ⓐ   Sold
   Ⓑ   Paid
   Ⓒ   New
   Ⓓ   Lost

Quiz 4: Use Homographs and Homophones

1. Which sentence is written correctly?

    Ⓐ   The puppies wagged their tales.

    Ⓑ   The puppies wagged there tales.

    Ⓒ   The puppies wagged their tails.

    Ⓓ   The puppies wagged there tails.

2. Which pair of words make the sentence correct?

    Shells from the _____ washed onto the _____.

    Ⓐ   see, sure

    Ⓑ   see, shore

    Ⓒ   sea, sure

    Ⓓ   sea, shore

3. In which sentence does skipped mean the same as below?

    Jan was busy, so she skipped breakfast.

    Ⓐ   Laura's sister skipped along the path.

    Ⓑ   Martin disliked the first song, so he skipped it.

    Ⓒ   Kevin hopped, skipped, and then jumped.

    Ⓓ   Anne skipped over the jump rope.

4 What does the word <u>wear</u> mean in the sentence?

The carpet was old and was starting to wear.

- Ⓐ To tire someone out
- Ⓑ To have clothing on
- Ⓒ To damage something by rubbing
- Ⓓ To pass time slowly

5 Read this sentence.

Carol dreams of having _____ that goes down to her _____.

Which pair of words make the sentence correct?
- Ⓐ hair, feet
- Ⓑ hair, feat
- Ⓒ hare, feet
- Ⓓ hare, feat

6 What does the word <u>present</u> mean in the sentence?

Mr. Johnson opened his birthday present.

- Ⓐ A gift
- Ⓑ To give something
- Ⓒ Taking place now
- Ⓓ To happen

Quiz 5: Understand and Use Prefixes

1. What does the word <u>resell</u> mean?

    Ⓐ Sell more

    Ⓑ Not sell

    Ⓒ Sell before

    Ⓓ Sell again

2. Which prefix can be added to the word <u>understand</u> to make a word meaning "not understand"?

    Ⓐ pre-

    Ⓑ re-

    Ⓒ mis-

    Ⓓ dis-

3. Which prefix should be added to the word to make the sentence correct?

    Greg __zipped his coat and took it off.

    Ⓐ un-

    Ⓑ dis-

    Ⓒ in-

    Ⓓ mis-

4. Which word below contains a prefix?

    Ⓐ Prepare

    Ⓑ President

    Ⓒ Pressure

    Ⓓ Precook

5   What does the word <u>dislike</u> mean?

   Ⓐ   Like more

   Ⓑ   Not like

   Ⓒ   Like before

   Ⓓ   Like again

6   Which prefix can be added to the word <u>kind</u> to make a word meaning "not kind"?

   Ⓐ   un-

   Ⓑ   in-

   Ⓒ   mis-

   Ⓓ   dis-

7   Which word means "pay before"?

   Ⓐ   Prepay

   Ⓑ   Repay

   Ⓒ   Mispay

   Ⓓ   Unpay

8   If a person is described as <u>impolite</u>, the person is —

   Ⓐ   rude

   Ⓑ   kind

   Ⓒ   careful

   Ⓓ   rash

Quiz 6: Understand and Use Suffixes

1. What does the word <u>loudest</u> mean?
   - Ⓐ Someone who is loud
   - Ⓑ More loud
   - Ⓒ The most loud
   - Ⓓ In a way that is loud

2. Which suffix can be added to the word <u>fear</u> to make a word meaning "without fear"?
   - Ⓐ -less
   - Ⓑ -ful
   - Ⓒ -ing
   - Ⓓ -ed

3. Which suffix should be added to the word to make the sentence correct?

   Corey neat___ folded his clothes.
   - Ⓐ -ful
   - Ⓑ -est
   - Ⓒ -er
   - Ⓓ -ly

4. The <u>en</u> in <u>thicken</u> means the same as the <u>en</u> in —
   - Ⓐ sudden
   - Ⓑ friend
   - Ⓒ soften
   - Ⓓ depend

5 What does the word <u>cheerful</u> mean?

- Ⓐ Having cheer
- Ⓑ The most cheer
- Ⓒ Someone who has cheer
- Ⓓ Less cheer

6 Which suffix can be added to the word <u>garden</u> to make a word meaning "one who gardens"?

- Ⓐ -er
- Ⓑ -ing
- Ⓒ -s
- Ⓓ -ed

7 If a situation is described as <u>harmful</u>, the situation is —

- Ⓐ safe
- Ⓑ dangerous
- Ⓒ exciting
- Ⓓ difficult

8 Which word correctly completes the sentence below?

Liam was amazed by the _____ of the stars in the sky.

- Ⓐ brightness
- Ⓑ brightly
- Ⓒ bright
- Ⓓ brighter

Section 3: Reading Practice Test 1

INTRODUCTION TO THE READING PRACTICE TEST
For Parents, Teachers, and Tutors

How Reading is Assessed by the State of Texas

The STAAR Reading test assesses reading skills by having students read literary and informational passages and answer questions about the passages. On the actual STAAR test, students will read 5 or 6 passages and answer 48 multiple-choice questions.

About the STAAR Reading Practice Test

This section of the book contains a practice test just like the real STAAR Reading test. It has 6 passages and a total of 48 multiple-choice questions. The questions cover all the skills tested on the STAAR Reading test, and have the same formats. Taking this practice test is just like taking the actual STAAR test.

Taking the Test

Students are given 4 hours to complete the actual STAAR Reading test. Individual schools are allowed to determine their own schedule, though the test must be completed on the same school day. Schools may choose to include breaks or to complete the test in two or more sessions.

This practice test is designed to be taken in two sessions of 2 hours each. You can use the same time limit, or you can choose not to time the test. In real testing situations, students will complete the two sessions on the same day. You can follow this schedule, or you can choose your own schedule.

Students complete the STAAR Reading test by marking their answers on an answer sheet. An answer sheet is included in the back of the book.

Reading Skills

The STAAR Reading test assesses a specific set of skills. These skills are described in the TEKS, or Texas Essential Knowledge and Skills. The full answer key at the end of the book identifies the specific skill that each question is testing.

STAAR Reading

Practice Test 1

Session 1

Instructions

Read the passages. Each passage is followed by questions.

Read each question carefully. Then select the best answer. Fill in the circle for the best answer.

Yard Sales

A yard sale is when you sell items in your front yard. People have yard sales to get rid of unwanted items. It does take some effort, but it's worth it. Here are some tips on how to have a good yard sale.

Finding the Items

1. You need a lot of items to sell. Search your home for all your unwanted items. Make sure everyone in the family joins in. Try to get a large range of items.

2. Clean out the garage or basement. Many people have a store of old stuff somewhere. Offer to clean up this area. As you do, collect everything you think you can sell.

3. Ask other people you know to join in. Many people have junk lying around they want to get rid of. They may be happy to give it to you to sell.

Setting It Up

1. Collect everything you have to sell. It is a good idea to make everything look neat and tidy. If you have clothes, wash them and hang them up. They may not be new clothes, but they'll have to look fresh and clean if you want people to buy them. Clean and dust all the items so they look their best.

2. Set up tables in your front yard to place all the items on. If you are placing items on the ground, put them on a sheet or blanket.

3. People will need to know how much each item is. Put a sticker on each item and write the price on it.

4. Collect some change. People will often pay in notes. Make sure you have plenty of coins to give as change.

Getting a Crowd

1. You want lots of people to come to your yard sale. Here are some things you should do:

- Tell all your friends
- Put notices on notice boards
- Put up flyers
- Put an ad in the local newspaper
- Put a sign at the end of your street

2. Make it easy for people to find the yard sale. Put balloons at the end of your street and in your front yard.

Time to Sell

1. Now it is time to sell your items. Remember that you are selling things you don't really want. Don't try to sell your items for too much. Be open to haggling too. Many people will want a bargain and may not want to pay what you think it's worth. If people suggest a lower price, take it! If people are thinking about buying something, make them a deal.

2. If items are not selling, lower the prices. It is better to sell items for something than to have to pack them all up again.

Popular Yard Sale Items
children's toys
clothes
building materials
furniture
kitchen items
books and movies

1 Read this sentence from the passage.

People often have yard sales to get rid of unwanted items.

What does the word <u>unwanted</u> mean?

Ⓐ Less wanted

Ⓑ Used to be wanted

Ⓒ More wanted

Ⓓ Not wanted

2 Why should you put balloons in your front yard?

Ⓐ So people feel good about buying

Ⓑ So you can sell them

Ⓒ So people can find your yard sale

Ⓓ So you can put prices on them

3 If the passage was given another title, which of these would best fit?

Ⓐ How to Make Money

Ⓑ How to Hold a Yard Sale

Ⓒ The Amazing Yard Sale

Ⓓ Cleaning Up Your House

4 Read this sentence from the passage.

It is a good idea to make everything look neat and tidy.

Which word means the opposite of <u>neat</u>?
- Ⓐ Messy
- Ⓑ Clean
- Ⓒ Dirty
- Ⓓ Nice

5 Which section of the passage describes how to let people know about your yard sale?
- Ⓐ Finding the Items
- Ⓑ Setting It Up
- Ⓒ Getting a Crowd
- Ⓓ Time to Sell

6 According to the passage, which of the following should you do first?
- Ⓐ Set up tables
- Ⓑ Clean all the items
- Ⓒ Put stickers on the items
- Ⓓ Lower the prices

7 How does the information in the table help the reader?

- Ⓐ It explains how much money can be made.
- Ⓑ It shows what sort of items to collect.
- Ⓒ It shows how to price items.
- Ⓓ It explains why you should have a yard sale.

8 Which phrase from "Time to Sell" best helps you understand the meaning of haggling?

- Ⓐ "now it is time"
- Ⓑ "things you don't really want"
- Ⓒ "suggest a lower price"
- Ⓓ "thinking about buying"

9 Which sentence from the first paragraph gives the main benefit of having a yard sale?

- Ⓐ *A yard sale is when you sell items in your front yard.*
- Ⓑ *People have yard sales to get rid of unwanted items.*
- Ⓒ *It does take some effort, but it's worth it.*
- Ⓓ *Here are some tips on how to have a good yard sale.*

The Wiggly Worm

The worm is one of nature's
most wonderful of creatures,
as it slinks beneath the soil,
with all its special features.

The worm is an explorer,
of both soft and well-worn land,
on a journey through the landscape,
unearthing stones, loose earth, and sand.

Though they barely see above the grass,
they see all beneath the ground,
hiding amongst the flower beds,
as they wiggle round and round.

Their bodies are long and slender
and as light as summer's breeze,
gilding shapes beneath the surface,
with slow and steady ease.

They're the envy of the rhino,
the hippopotamus, and ape,
and all the other animals that lack
one single beautiful shape.

So when you see the wiggly worm,
smile at his simple form,
and ponder his adventures,
in the earth all wet and warm.

10 In the line below, which word means the opposite of <u>beneath</u>?

they see all beneath the ground,

- Ⓐ Below
- Ⓑ Above
- Ⓒ Far
- Ⓓ Along

11 The poet would most likely describe worms as –

- Ⓐ scary
- Ⓑ amazing
- Ⓒ dirty
- Ⓓ boring

12 What is the rhyme pattern of each stanza of the poem?

- Ⓐ The second and fourth lines rhyme.
- Ⓑ There are two pairs of rhyming lines.
- Ⓒ The first and last lines rhyme.
- Ⓓ None of the lines rhyme.

13 Which line from the poem contains a simile?

- Ⓐ *as it slinks beneath the soil,*
- Ⓑ *hiding amongst the flower beds,*
- Ⓒ *and as light as summer's breeze,*
- Ⓓ *So when you see the wiggly worm,*

14 Which words from the poem describe what a worm looks like?

- Ⓐ *soft and well-worn*
- Ⓑ *long and slender*
- Ⓒ *slow and steady*
- Ⓓ *wet and warm*

15 Which literary device does the poet use in the line below?

in the earth all wet and warm.

- Ⓐ Simile
- Ⓑ Metaphor
- Ⓒ Alliteration
- Ⓓ Personification

16 According to the poem, why is the worm the envy of the rhino, hippopotamus, and ape?

- Ⓐ A worm has a more exciting life.
- Ⓑ A worm is able to hide underground.
- Ⓒ A worm has a simple body shape.
- Ⓓ A worm moves about by wiggling.

17 What does the poet mainly want readers to learn from the poem?

- Ⓐ Where worms can be found
- Ⓑ Why worms are useful
- Ⓒ How interesting worms are
- Ⓓ How worms are able to move

A Letter to My Favorite Author

July 1, 2013

Dear Simeon,

I am writing to tell you what a huge fan I am of your work. I have enjoyed your books since I was eight years old. I read a story in the newspaper that said you were ill. It made me feel sad. I wanted to write just to tell you how much I like your work. And that I hope you feel better soon too!

My love for your work began with your first book. *The Singing Swordfish* was so well-written. The pictures also helped to bring your words to life. I laughed so hard I cried the first time I read the book! From then on, I was hooked on your every word. I cannot imagine a better children's author existing anywhere else in the world. If there is one, I would certainly like to know about them too! If I had to choose which of your books was my favorite, it would be *The Shining Light*. That story was such an adventure from start to finish. Your book *Rainy Day* is also a favorite. It made me think a lot. And of course, I love *Just Lazing Around* as well. It always makes me laugh.

I hope that you feel better soon. You have given so much joy to so many people. Take care and thank you for all of the memories and moments of joy that you have given me.

Yours sincerely,

Kyle Harper

18 Read this sentence from the letter.

   From then on, I was hooked on your every word.

   What does the phrase "hooked on" mean?

   Ⓐ Very keen on
   Ⓑ Confused by
   Ⓒ Bent
   Ⓓ Owned

19 In the sentence below, which word means about the same as <u>existing</u>?

   I cannot imagine a better children's author existing anywhere else in the world.

   Ⓐ Living
   Ⓑ Writing
   Ⓒ Working
   Ⓓ Thinking

20 According to the letter, why does Kyle decide to write to Simeon?

   Ⓐ He is asked to by his mother.
   Ⓑ He wants to be sent a free book.
   Ⓒ He wants her to write another book.
   Ⓓ He reads that she is ill.

21 Which book did Kyle read first?

- Ⓐ *Just Lazing Around*
- Ⓑ *Rainy Day*
- Ⓒ *The Shining Light*
- Ⓓ *The Singing Swordfish*

22 The reader can tell that Kyle —

- Ⓐ no longer reads Simeon's books
- Ⓑ wants to be a writer someday
- Ⓒ has read many of Simeon's books
- Ⓓ started reading because he was ill

23 What is the first paragraph mainly about?

- Ⓐ Why Kyle is writing to Simeon
- Ⓑ When Kyle started reading Simeon's books
- Ⓒ Which book of Simeon's is Kyle's favorite
- Ⓓ How Kyle reads the newspaper

24 Which part of the letter tells who wrote the letter?

- Ⓐ Date
- Ⓑ Greeting
- Ⓒ Closing
- Ⓓ Body

END OF SESSION 1

STAAR Reading

Practice Test 1

Session 2

Instructions

Read the passages. Each passage is followed by questions.

Read each question carefully. Then select the best answer. Fill in the circle for the best answer.

The Troublemaker

Kevin had always been known for playing tricks. As he got older, his tricks got worse. Over time, everyone began to know Kevin as a troublemaker. Kevin enjoyed all of the attention. He almost felt famous for his tricks.

One day, he was at his friend Jason's house playing hide and seek. Kevin told Jason to hide from the others in his basement. Jason opened the door and started down the steps. Kevin quickly locked the basement door behind him. Kevin put the key into his pocket and skipped away.

Jason called out to his friends. He couldn't hear a reply, so he called out a little louder. He rattled the doorknob hoping it would open. Then he began banging on the door. Jason's friends heard the sound and raced to the door. They called out to let Jason know they would get him out soon. Jason's friend Max pushed on the door as hard as he could. But the door would not budge.

Eventually, Jason's mother heard the noise and came downstairs. She unlocked the door with a spare key and hugged her son as he ran out.

"Who did this?" she asked firmly.

Kevin smiled and put his hand in the air. Jason's mother sighed.

"You seem very proud, Kevin," she said. "But what you don't realize is that being well-known for something isn't always a good thing. Maybe once you were thought of as funny, but now you're just becoming nasty."

Kevin's shoulders slumped.

"I guess so," he whispered. "I just thought it would be funny. I didn't mean to hurt anybody. But I guess nobody is laughing, are they?"

Kevin decided he would have to be more careful about the jokes he chose to play on his friends.

25 Read these sentences from the passage.

> **Jason's friend Max pushed on the door as hard as he could. But the door would not budge.**

What does the word <u>budge</u> mean in the sentence?
- Ⓐ Break
- Ⓑ Bend
- Ⓒ Move
- Ⓓ Listen

26 Which two words from the passage have about the same meaning?
- Ⓐ *friends, relatives*
- Ⓑ *naughty, tricks*
- Ⓒ *proud, nice*
- Ⓓ *famous, well-known*

27 Who is the main character in the passage?
- Ⓐ Kevin
- Ⓑ Jason's mother
- Ⓒ Jason
- Ⓓ Max

28 Read this sentence from the passage.

Kevin put the key into his pocket and skipped away.

What does the word <u>skipped</u> suggest about Kevin?

- Ⓐ He moved slowly.
- Ⓑ He was happy.
- Ⓒ He moved quietly.
- Ⓓ He was angry.

29 What happens right after Jason's mother comes downstairs?

- Ⓐ She asks who locked Jason in the basement.
- Ⓑ She lets Jason out of the basement.
- Ⓒ She explains to Kevin why he should not play tricks.
- Ⓓ She hears a noise coming from the basement.

30 Which word best describes the trick that Kevin plays on Jason?

- Ⓐ Funny
- Ⓑ Mean
- Ⓒ Strange
- Ⓓ Silly

31 What is the second paragraph mostly about?

Ⓐ Why Kevin plays tricks

Ⓑ How children should not play in basements

Ⓒ A trick that Kevin plays on a friend

Ⓓ How a boy learns why he shouldn't play tricks

32 Which word describes how Jason feels while he is locked in the basement?

Ⓐ Calm

Ⓑ Bored

Ⓒ Angry

Ⓓ Frightened

33 Which sentence from the third paragraph best supports your answer to Question 32?

Ⓐ *Jason called out to his friends.*

Ⓑ *Then he began banging on the door.*

Ⓒ *Jason's friends heard the sound and raced to the door.*

Ⓓ *But the door would not budge.*

The New York Times

The New York Times is an American newspaper. It was founded in New York. It was first printed in 1851. The first issue cost just 1 cent to buy. It is printed each day. Each issue is read by around one million people. The newspaper has won over 110 Pulitzer Prizes. A Pulitzer Prize is an award given for excellent reporting. This is more than any other newspaper or magazine.

The New York Times is the largest local newspaper in the United States. It is also the third largest newspaper overall. Only *The Wall Street Journal* and *USA Today* are read by more people.

Even though it is still popular, it sells fewer copies today than in the past. In 1990, it was read by over a million people. By 2010, it was being read by less than a million people. This change has occurred for most printed newspapers. The main reason is that people can read the news on the Internet for free.

The newspaper's motto is "All the News That's Fit to Print." This appears printed in the top corner of the front page.

The newspaper has many different sections. It covers news, business, and science. It also covers sport, home, and fashion. It has sections for travel, food, art, and movies. It is also known for its difficult crossword puzzles.

In 2011, each issue sold for $2. However, the Sunday issue is larger. It is sold for $5.

At the offices of *The New York Times*, hundreds of people work to create the newspaper every day.

34 What does the word <u>founded</u> mean in the sentence?

It was founded in New York.

- Ⓐ Sold
- Ⓑ Discovered
- Ⓒ Started
- Ⓓ Lost

35 As it is used in the sentence below, what does <u>fit</u> mean?

The newspaper's motto is "All the News That's Fit to Print."

- Ⓐ Ready
- Ⓑ Healthy
- Ⓒ Right
- Ⓓ Known

36 According to the passage, how is *The Wall Street Journal* different from *The New York Times*?

- Ⓐ It is read by more people.
- Ⓑ It has won more awards.
- Ⓒ It costs less to buy.
- Ⓓ It has fewer sections.

37 According to the passage, why are fewer copies of *The New York Times* sold today than in the past?

- Ⓐ It costs too much.
- Ⓑ People read the news online.
- Ⓒ People buy other newspapers instead.
- Ⓓ It has too many sections.

38 The photograph mainly suggests that the offices of *The New York Times* are —

- Ⓐ serious and gloomy
- Ⓑ old and dated
- Ⓒ busy and lively
- Ⓓ fresh and modern

39 Which detail best shows that *The New York Times* is successful?

- Ⓐ It is printed seven days a week.
- Ⓑ Its price has increased to $2.
- Ⓒ It has a motto.
- Ⓓ It has won over 110 Pulitzer Prizes.

40 The web below summarizes information from the passage.

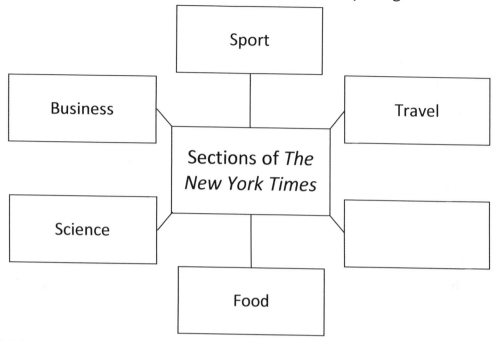

Which word best completes the web?

Ⓐ Gardening
Ⓑ Comics
Ⓒ Music
Ⓓ Movies

41 In which sentence does <u>free</u> mean the same as in the sentence below?

The main reason is that people can read the news on the Internet for free.

Ⓐ Jorja gave the kitten away for <u>free</u>.
Ⓑ Andy was happy to have the whole day <u>free</u>.
Ⓒ The diner was so busy that only one table was <u>free</u>.
Ⓓ The beach always made Kyle feel relaxed and <u>free</u>.

A Bold Decision

Steven loved playing for his basketball team. He had been playing basketball for as long as he could remember. Last year, they had won the state finals. This year, they were finding things much harder. There were only three games left in the season. Steven's team needed to win them all if they were going to the state playoffs. It was near the end of the game. They were behind by six points. Steven had just saved a basket with a great block. But he had hurt his knee as he landed.

"Are you okay to play?" asked his coach.

Steven frowned at the pain in his knee.

"I'll be fine," he said.

Steven knew the risks of his decision. He could risk hurting his knee even more. Or he could choose not to play. He knew that not playing might cause his team to lose. As he rested before the final quarter, he decided to play through the pain. He was going to win this game for the team he loved.

As the quarter started, he caught the ball after the other team made a mistake. He bounced the ball down the court and threw the ball into the hoop. Steven smiled towards his coach on the sidelines. They were only four points behind now.

Steven kept playing well during the final quarter. He even scored a three point shot from the center of the court. With just two minutes left on the clock, Steven's team was only one point behind. Steven was passed the ball by his teammate. He ignored the pain in his knee and sprinted forward. He headed towards the end of the court. His feet left the ground. He sent his shot into the basket and earned his side two points. The final whistle blew seconds after. Steven's bold decision had won his team the game.

42 In the sentence below, which word could best be used in place of <u>center</u>?

He even scored a three point shot from the center of the court.

- Ⓐ Edge
- Ⓑ Middle
- Ⓒ Back
- Ⓓ Front

43 Which pair of sentences from the first paragraph best tell why the game is important to Steven?

- Ⓐ *Last year, they had won the state finals. This year, they were finding things much harder.*
- Ⓑ *There were only three games left in the season. Steven's team needed to win them all if they were going to the state playoffs.*
- Ⓒ *It was near the end of the game. They were behind by six points.*
- Ⓓ *Steven had just saved a basket with a great block. But he had hurt his knee as he landed.*

44 Read this sentence from the passage.

He ignored the pain in his knee and sprinted forward.

The word <u>sprinted</u> shows that Steven moved —

- Ⓐ quickly
- Ⓑ shakily
- Ⓒ quietly
- Ⓓ slowly

45 What is Steven's bold decision?
- Ⓐ Deciding to play when he is hurt
- Ⓑ Deciding to take the final shot
- Ⓒ Deciding to win the game
- Ⓓ Deciding to try to make a three point shot

46 Why does Steven decide to play?
- Ⓐ He really wants his team to win.
- Ⓑ He does not want to upset his coach.
- Ⓒ He does not realize that he is hurt.
- Ⓓ He wants everyone to cheer for him.

47 What is the last paragraph mainly about?
- Ⓐ How Steven's team won the game
- Ⓑ How Steven felt at the end of the game
- Ⓒ Why the game was important to Steven
- Ⓓ How to shoot a basket correctly

48 The author would probably describe Steven as –
- Ⓐ kind
- Ⓑ clever
- Ⓒ silly
- Ⓓ brave

END OF SESSION 2

Section 4: Reading Practice Test 2

INTRODUCTION TO THE READING PRACTICE TEST
For Parents, Teachers, and Tutors

How Reading is Assessed by the State of Texas

The STAAR Reading test assesses reading skills by having students read literary and informational passages and answer questions about the passages. On the actual STAAR test, students will read 5 or 6 passages and answer 48 multiple-choice questions.

About the STAAR Reading Practice Test

This section of the book contains a practice test just like the real STAAR Reading test. It has 6 passages and a total of 48 multiple-choice questions. The questions cover all the skills tested on the STAAR Reading test, and have the same formats. Taking this practice test is just like taking the actual STAAR test.

Taking the Test

Students are given 4 hours to complete the actual STAAR Reading test. Individual schools are allowed to determine their own schedule, though the test must be completed on the same school day. Schools may choose to include breaks or to complete the test in two or more sessions.

This practice test is designed to be taken in two sessions of 2 hours each. You can use the same time limit, or you can choose not to time the test. In real testing situations, students will complete the two sessions on the same day. You can follow this schedule, or you can choose your own schedule.

Students complete the STAAR Reading test by marking their answers on an answer sheet. An answer sheet is included in the back of the book.

Reading Skills

The STAAR Reading test assesses a specific set of skills. These skills are described in the TEKS, or Texas Essential Knowledge and Skills. The full answer key at the end of the book identifies the specific skill that each question is testing.

STAAR Reading

Practice Test 2

Session 1

Instructions

Read the passages. Each passage is followed by questions.

Read each question carefully. Then select the best answer. Fill in the circle for the best answer.

No Time to Talk

May 23, 2013

Dear Principal Becker,

I understand that school is meant for learning. It is important to have good reading skills and to be able to solve math problems. But I think school is also important for another reason. It helps people learn to get along with others.

It may seem like lunchtime is not important. After all, I spend most lunchtimes just chatting to my friends. But this activity is more important than it looks.

I am learning how to get along with others. I am learning how to solve problems. I am finding out new things from people, and realizing my mistakes. I am learning how to stand up for myself. I am learning how to say sorry. These are all important skills to learn.

My problem is that the time for lunch and our other breaks keep getting shorter. I know this is happening so we can spend more time in class learning. But please do not forget that we are also learning in our lunchtimes. We are learning people skills. It is important that we have enough time to spend with our friends.

I ask that you consider making our lunch break longer. A little more time spent with friends each day would benefit everybody.

Best,

Simone Anderson

1 Read this sentence from the letter.

> **My problem is that the time for lunch and our other breaks keep getting shorter.**

What does the word <u>shorter</u> mean?

- Ⓐ Less short
- Ⓑ The most short
- Ⓒ More short
- Ⓓ The least short

2 What does the word <u>benefit</u> mean in the sentence below?

> **A little more time spent with friends each day would benefit everybody.**

- Ⓐ Change
- Ⓑ Help
- Ⓒ Interest
- Ⓓ Harm

3 According to the letter, what does Simone learn at lunchtime?

- Ⓐ Math skills
- Ⓑ Reading skills
- Ⓒ People skills
- Ⓓ Drawing skills

4 Why did Simone write the letter?

- Ⓐ To persuade the principal to do something
- Ⓑ To entertain the principal
- Ⓒ To show the principal her writing skills
- Ⓓ To teach the principal how to do something

5 Which sentence best shows the main idea of the letter?

- Ⓐ *I understand that school is meant for learning.*
- Ⓑ *It may seem like lunchtime is not important.*
- Ⓒ *After all, I spend most lunchtimes just chatting to my friends.*
- Ⓓ *It is important that we have enough time to spend with our friends.*

6 What is the paragraph below mostly about?

> **I am learning how to get along with others. I am learning how to solve problems. I am finding out new things from people, and realizing my mistakes. I am learning how to stand up for myself. I am learning how to say sorry. These are all important skills to learn.**

- Ⓐ What Simone learns at lunchtime
- Ⓑ How long lunchtime lasts for
- Ⓒ What skills students should be taught
- Ⓓ What problems Simone has each day

7 Look at the web below.

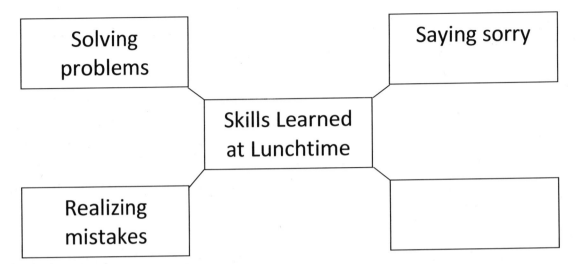

Which of these best completes the web?

Ⓐ Solving math problems
Ⓑ Standing up for yourself
Ⓒ Managing time
Ⓓ Reading well

8 Which statement is most likely true about Simone?

Ⓐ She writes a lot of letters to the principal.
Ⓑ She spends a lot of time in class talking.
Ⓒ She enjoys spending time with her friends.
Ⓓ She wishes that her friends were nicer.

Sarah and Janet

Sarah and her sister Janet were always competing with each other. Sarah always wanted to outdo Janet. Janet always wanted to outdo Sarah.

They liked most of the same things and this often led to fights. If Janet sang a song, Sarah wanted to sing it louder and better. If Sarah learned a new song on the piano, Janet had to learn it too and she would try to perform it better. They both wanted to be the fastest runner and the best volleyball player. They would even compete over who could finish reading a book the fastest. It drove their mother crazy.

"Why can't you girls just get along?" she would ask them time and time again. "I am so tired of hearing your bickering."

They would just shrug and keep on arguing. One day, their mother had an idea to help them get along. She planned to take them shopping at the local mall. The girls were excited about taking a shopping trip.

"Now you can both pick out something," said their mother as she parked the car outside the mall. "But choose carefully because you can each only have one outfit."

When they arrived at the mall, they entered a clothing shop. Soon enough, the girls began fighting over the clothing.

"I want this dress," Sarah stated.

"No, I want that dress," Janet said.

"I'm having it because it'll look better on me," Sarah said.

"It will not! It will look better on me," Janet said.

"Alright," said their mother quietly. "Since you both like the dress so much, you can both have one. But do you want to each pick a different color?"

"I want the blue one," Sarah quickly stated.

"No, you should get the yellow one. It would look so nice on you," Janet replied.

"You just want me to get the yellow one because you want the blue one," Sarah argued. "But I'm not being fooled. I'm getting the blue one and you can choose whatever one you want."

"Fine. Then I'm getting the blue one too."

Their mother sighed and took the two blue dresses up to the counter. She handed both Sarah and Janet their new dress and they all left the store.

The girls looked at each other. They were both confused. Usually their mother would buy them different clothes. She had never bought them the same thing before. They were happy to get what they wanted, but they returned home unsure as to what was happening.

It all became clear the following day. The girls dressed for school in their own rooms and headed downstairs for breakfast. They were shocked to see that they were both wearing the same outfit. They began to argue about who should go and change their clothes.

"Nobody is going to change their clothes," said their mother. "You both chose these clothes, so you can both wear them. Now you can see what your silly arguments have led to."

The girls giggled as they realized what their mother was saying.

9 What does the word bickering mean in the sentence below?

"I am so tired of hearing your bickering."

- Ⓐ   Arguing
- Ⓑ   Complaining
- Ⓒ   Singing
- Ⓓ   Competing

10 Which meaning of the word clear is used in the sentence below?

It all became clear the following day.

- Ⓐ   Able to be seen through
- Ⓑ   Fine or nice
- Ⓒ   Understood or known
- Ⓓ   Sounding pleasant

11 What is the mother's main problem in the passage?
- Ⓐ   Her daughters have too many things.
- Ⓑ   Her daughters need more clothes.
- Ⓒ   Her daughters wear the same outfits.
- Ⓓ   Her daughters are always fighting.

12 Which sentence spoken by the mother best supports your answer to Question 11?

- Ⓐ "Why can't you girls just get along?"
- Ⓑ "But choose carefully because you can each only have one outfit."
- Ⓒ "But do you want to each pick a different color?"
- Ⓓ "You both chose these clothes, so you can both wear them."

13 Read this sentence from the passage.

> **"Why can't you girls just get along?" she would ask them time and time again.**

What does the phrase "time and time again" suggest?

- Ⓐ That the mother has asked the question for the last time
- Ⓑ That the mother asks at the same time each day
- Ⓒ That the mother has asked the question many times
- Ⓓ That the mother asked the question once an hour

14 Where would this passage most likely be found?

- Ⓐ In a book of poems
- Ⓑ In a magazine
- Ⓒ In a science textbook
- Ⓓ In a book of short stories

15 What happens right after the girls come downstairs for breakfast?

- Ⓐ They see that they are wearing the same thing.
- Ⓑ They begin to argue.
- Ⓒ They start giggling.
- Ⓓ They get dressed for school.

16 If the passage was given another title, which title would best fit?

- Ⓐ Being Your Best
- Ⓑ How to Shop Well
- Ⓒ Fighting Over Nothing
- Ⓓ The Magic Dress

17 What most likely happens next in the passage?

- Ⓐ The girls go shopping again
- Ⓑ The girls go to school looking the same
- Ⓒ The girls put on a different matching outfit
- Ⓓ The girls ask their father for help

Summer Lemonade

Lemonade is one of the most popular summer drinks in the United States. It is refreshing and helps you to cool down during the hot summer months. Lemonade is available in most stores and can be purchased as a premade drink. These brands are often made with added sugar and other chemicals. These ingredients often make the drink unhealthy. So we're going to make a healthy homemade lemonade!

To make our own lemonade at home we'll need the right ingredients. You will need 1 cup of sugar, 6 lemons, 1 cup of boiling water, and 4 cups of cold water. You will also need a saucepan and a large pitcher.

Step 1
Start by placing the sugar in a saucepan. Then add the boiling water and heat the mixture gently.

Step 2
Extract the juice from your 6 lemons. You can use a juicer. Or you can squeeze them by hand. Add the lemon juice to the water and sugar mixture.

Step 3
Pour the mixture into a pitcher. Then take your 4 cups of cold water and add these to the pitcher. This will cool the mixture down and make it ready to refrigerate. The amount of cold water that you add will affect the strength of the lemonade. You can add more water if you like it weaker.

Step 4
Refrigerate the mixture for 30 or 40 minutes. Taste your lemonade mixture. If it is too sweet, add a little more lemon juice. If it is too strong, add some more water. If it is too sour, add some more sugar.

Step 5
You are now ready to serve your lemonade. Pour it into a glass with ice and a slice of lemon.

Now that you know how to make lemonade, why not use this new skill to make some money on the weekend? Make a nice big batch of lemonade and start a lemonade stand in your front yard. Here are some tips for setting up a good lemonade stand.

1. Make sure you have a good spot. You're usually not allowed to set up stands in public places like parks, so you'll need to do it in your yard. But it's best if you live in a spot where plenty of people will walk past. If your home is not right, consider asking a friend who lives in a better spot to help you. Then you can set up the stand at your friend's house.

2. Get your stand noticed. You want your stand to be easy to spot. Take the time to paint a colorful banner or to put up signs. You can also add things like streamers and balloons. You could also put signs up at the end of your street. Then people will know that fresh lemonade is just around the corner.

3. Choose the right price. You need to make sure you aren't charging too much for your lemonade. It's also easiest if you don't need to worry about giving change. Set your price to $1, $2, or $3. You should also be willing to do deals. If someone wants to buy more than one, offer them a special deal.

4. You want people to want to drink your lemonade, so make sure you present it nicely. You can add a few lemon wedges to the container to make it look nice and fresh. You can also place lemons around your stand as decorations. You should also cover the table you are using with a nice tablecloth. The nicer your stand looks, the more people will want to buy your product.

5. Add other products. Do you have a friend who makes delicious cupcakes or amazing banana bread? Invite them to join in. You can sell treats to go with your fresh lemonade and make even more money.

18 In the sentence below, what does the word <u>premade</u> mean?

Lemonade is available in most stores and can be purchased as a <u>premade</u> drink.

- Ⓐ Poorly made
- Ⓑ Carefully made
- Ⓒ Already made
- Ⓓ Not yet made

19 What would be the best way to improve how the information in paragraph 2 is presented?

- Ⓐ Add bullet points
- Ⓑ Add a diagram
- Ⓒ Add a chart
- Ⓓ Add a graph

20 What is the main purpose of the first paragraph?

- Ⓐ To describe how to make lemonade
- Ⓑ To encourage people to want to make lemonade
- Ⓒ To tell what lemonade is made from
- Ⓓ To explain where to get lemonade from

21 What is one reason the author gives for asking a friend to help with the lemonade stand?

- Ⓐ The friend could make sure the lemonade tastes good.
- Ⓑ You could set up the stand at the friend's house.
- Ⓒ The friend could help you make the lemonade.
- Ⓓ You could have your friend take care of giving change.

22 As it is used below, which word means the opposite of <u>weaker</u>?

You can add more water if you like it weaker.

Ⓐ Nicer

Ⓑ Stronger

Ⓒ Thinner

Ⓓ Colder

23 Which sentence completes the empty box in the diagram below?

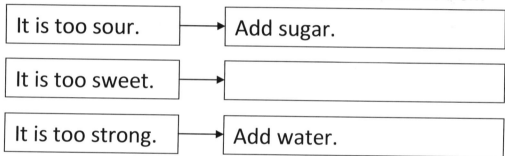

Problem with the Lemonade **How to Solve the Problem**

It is too sour. → Add sugar.

It is too sweet. →

It is too strong. → Add water.

Ⓐ Add more lemon juice.

Ⓑ Put in some lemon wedges.

Ⓒ Add a small amount of salt.

Ⓓ Cool the lemonade.

24 According to the passage, why is homemade lemonade better than lemonade from a store?

Ⓐ It lasts longer.

Ⓑ It is cheaper.

Ⓒ It is better for you.

Ⓓ It is easier to make.

END OF SESSION 1

STAAR Reading

Practice Test 2

Session 2

Instructions

Read the passages. Each passage is followed by questions.

Read each question carefully. Then select the best answer. Fill in the circle for the best answer.

The Bumble Bee

Yellow and black with a set of tiny wings,
I busily buzz around the land,
And boast a mighty sting!

I do not care for fame or money,
I do not wish to harm,
I just live for making honey!

This beekeeper holds up honeycomb that has been made in the hive. The honey is extracted, or taken out, from the honeycomb. Bees can sting, so this beekeeper wears a special bee suit to keep him safe. Bees usually only sting when they are afraid of something. The best way to be safe from bees is simply to leave them alone!

25 According to the poem, what does the bee enjoy most?

- Ⓐ Being famous
- Ⓑ Being rich
- Ⓒ Making honey
- Ⓓ Stinging people

26 Read this line from the poem.

> **I busily buzz around the land,**

Which literary device is used in this line?

- Ⓐ Alliteration
- Ⓑ Simile
- Ⓒ Metaphor
- Ⓓ Imagery

27 What is the rhyme pattern of each stanza of the poem?

- Ⓐ Every line rhymes.
- Ⓑ The first and second lines rhyme.
- Ⓒ The first and last lines rhyme.
- Ⓓ None of the lines rhyme.

28 Onomatopoeia is when a word sounds like what it describes. Which word from the poem is an example of onomatopoeia?

- Ⓐ *black*
- Ⓑ *wings*
- Ⓒ *buzz*
- Ⓓ *sting*

29 In the line below, what does the word <u>mighty</u> mean?

And boast a mighty sting!

- Ⓐ   Scary
- Ⓑ   Strange
- Ⓒ   Naughty
- Ⓓ   Great

30 Which sentence from the caption best supports the idea that bees do not wish to harm?

- Ⓐ   *This beekeeper holds up honeycomb that has been made in the hive.*
- Ⓑ   *The honey is extracted, or taken out, from the honeycomb.*
- Ⓒ   *Bees can sting, so this beekeeper wears a special bee suit to keep him safe.*
- Ⓓ   *Bees usually only sting when they are afraid of something.*

31 What does the photograph mainly help readers understand?

- Ⓐ   How bees have a powerful sting that can harm
- Ⓑ   Why bees make honey
- Ⓒ   What to do if you are stung by a bee
- Ⓓ   Where bees are found in the wild

The Shining Light Day Center

As parents, the wellbeing of your children is very important. It is important to keep them happy and healthy. It is also important to make sure their bodies and minds are active. It is especially important for children under the age of five. During this time, children can learn good fitness habits that they will keep for life.

During this time, children also learn quickly. They are at a special age where they take in information quickly. They also develop skills easier. It is important to find time to develop both their bodies and minds.

As parents, it can be hard to find time for all this. At the Shining Light Day Center, we understand this. We have created a range of activities to help your child.

Our activities cover many different areas. We want to help children think and learn. We want to help children learn to work with others. We want to help children learn to read and speak. We also want to help children be fit and healthy. Our activities include classes, games, and time for free play. These keep the child interested. At the same time, they are learning and growing.

Our programs are aimed at children between the ages of 3 and 5. Children will enjoy playing with others. They will learn basic math and English skills. Our program helps children start grade school. Think of it as a head start for your child!

Our classes are held at two different times. On weekdays, classes are held from noon to 3 p.m. On weekends, classes are held from 9 to 11 a.m. This gives you a lot of choice as a parent. You can choose the day and time that best suits you.

All parents should consider the Shining Light Day Center. It will give your child the best head start in life. Visit our website today to learn more. You can also call a member of our staff to discuss your child's future. You can also drop in any time to watch a class.

Learning Activity	Details
Storytelling	Children listen to stories being told. They answer questions about the story. Then they help write the ending to the story.
Telling Time	Students learn counting skills by using clocks. They count hours and minutes.
Hide and Seek	Children must find blocks hidden in our outdoor play areas. They race to find all the blocks of their color.
Puppet Show	Children use hand puppets to act out stories. They work in pairs.

32 Read this sentence from the passage.

They also develop skills easier.

Which word means the opposite of <u>easier</u>?
- Ⓐ Simpler
- Ⓑ Harder
- Ⓒ Quicker
- Ⓓ Slower

33 Which two words from the passage have about the same meaning?
- Ⓐ *read, speak*
- Ⓑ *fit, healthy*
- Ⓒ *day, time*
- Ⓓ *learning, school*

34 The passage is most like –
- Ⓐ an essay
- Ⓑ an advertisement
- Ⓒ a short story
- Ⓓ a news article

35 How is the third paragraph mainly organized?
- Ⓐ A problem is described and then a solution is given.
- Ⓑ Events are described in the order they occur.
- Ⓒ Facts are given to support an argument.
- Ⓓ A question is asked and then answered.

36 In the sentence below, what do the words "drop in" mean?

You can also drop in any time to watch a class.

- Ⓐ Phone
- Ⓑ Check
- Ⓒ Visit
- Ⓓ Watch

37 The passage was probably written mainly to –
- Ⓐ encourage parents to send their children to the day center
- Ⓑ compare the day center with grade school
- Ⓒ describe why the day center was started
- Ⓓ inform parents about the benefits of learning

38 Which sentence is included mainly to persuade the reader?
- Ⓐ *As parents, it can be hard to find time for all this.*
- Ⓑ *Our programs are aimed at children between the ages of 3 and 5.*
- Ⓒ *On weekdays, classes are held from noon to 3 p.m.*
- Ⓓ *It will give your child the best head start in life.*

39 Which activity from the table would be most likely to develop math skills?

Ⓐ Storytelling

Ⓑ Telling Time

Ⓒ Hide and Seek

Ⓓ Puppet Show

40 Look at the web below.

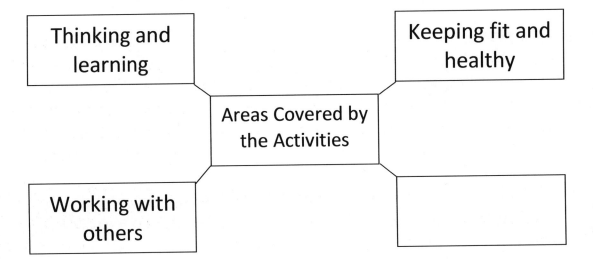

Which of these best completes the web?

Ⓐ Reading and speaking

Ⓑ Solving problems

Ⓒ Understanding shapes

Ⓓ Making decisions

A Special Day

Dear Uncle Yuri,

Today was quite an amazing day for me. It was the day that my father returned home from overseas. He had been away from us for over a year. He was chosen to work on a special research project in London. He and his team were working on a new way to make recycled paper products. It would use less water and energy and be better for the environment. Although we were proud of him, we longed for the day when he would wake up under the same roof as us. We had missed him more than words could ever say. Now the day had finally arrived. He had worked hard and it was time for him to return home.

Mom woke us at 6 a.m. to head to the airport. My father's flight was due in at 9:30. "We don't want to be late!" she kept saying as she woke everyone up. She had no need to remind me! I quickly dressed, washed, and made my way downstairs for breakfast. I could not take my eyes off the clock all morning. Time was going so slowly. When the clock struck 8:45, my mom told us all it was time to go. We all raced to the car and made our way quickly to the airport.

We arrived just after 9 and hurried to the terminal to wait. But 9:30 came and went and our father's flight had still not arrived. Another 10 minutes went by, and I started pacing up and down. I kept asking Mom where he was. She just kept smiling and saying he'd be there soon. I searched the crowds of people, hoping to see his familiar face. I stood as tall as I could to try and see every person coming through the gate.

Then suddenly a gap appeared in the crowd and a tall shadow emerged. There was my father standing before me. He dropped his bags to the floor and swept my sister and I up in his arms. "I've missed you so much," he said through tears of joy. We all cried together. I never want my father to ever let me go.

Today was pretty perfect.

Holly

41 Read this sentence from the letter.

I could not take my eyes off the clock all morning.

This sentence shows that Holly was –

Ⓐ worried

Ⓑ excited

Ⓒ bored

Ⓓ patient

42 Why does Holly most likely say that she doesn't need to be reminded not to be late?

Ⓐ She does not care if they are late.

Ⓑ She knows that the plane will be late.

Ⓒ She would never want to be late.

Ⓓ She thinks that they will be late anyway.

43 The second paragraph starts with the sentence "Mom woke us at 6 a.m. to head to the airport." How is the second paragraph mainly organized?

Ⓐ A problem is described and then a solution is given.

Ⓑ Events are described in the order they occur.

Ⓒ Facts are given to support an argument.

Ⓓ A question is asked and then answered.

44 The reader can tell that Holly's father —
- Ⓐ missed his family very much
- Ⓑ wants to go overseas again
- Ⓒ is surprised to be home
- Ⓓ thinks his kids have grown up a lot

45 How does Holly most likely feel while waiting at the airport?
- Ⓐ Surprised
- Ⓑ Anxious
- Ⓒ Calm
- Ⓓ Bored

46 Which sentence from the letter best shows how Holly feels about having her father home?
- Ⓐ *There was my father standing before me.*
- Ⓑ *He dropped his bags to the floor and swept my sister and I up in his arms.*
- Ⓒ *We all cried together.*
- Ⓓ *I never want my father to ever let me go.*

47 Which sentence from the letter best explains why Holly is looking forward to seeing her father so much?

Ⓐ   *Today was quite an amazing day for me.*

Ⓑ   *He had been away from us for over a year.*

Ⓒ   *My father's flight was due in at 9:30.*

Ⓓ   *Time was going so slowly.*

48 The photograph in the passage mainly helps show that the airport was —

Ⓐ   clean

Ⓑ   loud

Ⓒ   crowded

Ⓓ   cold

END OF SESSION 2

ANSWER KEY

The STAAR Reading test assesses a specific set of skills. These are described in the Texas Essential Knowledge and Skills, or TEKS. The TEKS are the state standards that describe what students should know and what students should be able to do.

The questions in this book cover all the TEKS standards that are assessed on the state test. The answer key that follows includes the TEKS standard that each question is testing. Use the skill listed with each question to identify areas of strength and weakness. Then target revision and instruction accordingly.

Section 1: Reading Mini-Tests

Mini-Test 1, Literary Text

Question	Answer	TEKS Standard
1	C	Use context to determine the relevant meaning of unfamiliar words or distinguish among multiple meaning words and homographs.
2	B	Ask relevant questions, seek clarification, and locate facts and details about stories and other texts and support answers with evidence from text.
3	D	Sequence and summarize the plot's main events and explain their influence on future events.
4	C	Describe the interaction of characters including their relationships and the changes they undergo.
5	A	Identify language that creates a graphic visual experience and appeals to the senses.
6	D	Identify and use antonyms, synonyms, homographs, and homophones.
7	B	Paraphrase the themes and supporting details of fables, legends, myths, or stories.
8	C	Use context to determine the relevant meaning of unfamiliar words or distinguish among multiple meaning words and homographs.
9	C	Make inferences about text and use textual evidence to support understanding.
10	D	Use comprehension skills to analyze how words, images, graphics, and sounds work together in various forms to impact meaning.

Mini-Test 2, Informational Text

Question	Answer	TEKS Standard
1	B	Use context to determine the relevant meaning of unfamiliar words or distinguish among multiple meaning words and homographs.
2	B	Use text features (e.g., bold print, captions, key words, italics) to locate information and make and verify predictions about contents of text.
3	A	Draw conclusions from the facts presented in text and support those assertions with textual evidence.
4	A	Summarize information in text, maintaining meaning and logical order.
5	B	Use context to determine the relevant meaning of unfamiliar words or distinguish among multiple meaning words and homographs.
6	C	Use text features (e.g., bold print, captions, key words, italics) to locate information and make and verify predictions about contents of text.
7	C	Use comprehension skills to analyze how words, images, graphics, and sounds work together in various forms to impact meaning.
8	B	Locate and use specific information in graphic features of text.
9	A	Identify explicit cause and effect relationships among ideas in texts.
10	D	Summarize information in text, maintaining meaning and logical order.

Mini-Test 3, Literary Text

Question	Answer	TEKS Standard
1	B	Use context to determine the relevant meaning of unfamiliar words or distinguish among multiple meaning words and homographs.
2	C	Use context to determine the relevant meaning of unfamiliar words or distinguish among multiple meaning words and homographs.
3	A	Describe the characteristics of various forms of poetry and how they create imagery (e.g., narrative poetry, lyrical poetry, humorous poetry, free verse).
4	A	Identify language that creates a graphic visual experience and appeals to the senses.
5	C	Describe the characteristics of various forms of poetry and how they create imagery (e.g., narrative poetry, lyrical poetry, humorous poetry, free verse).
6	C	Summarize information in text, maintaining meaning and logical order.
7	A	Paraphrase the themes and supporting details of fables, legends, myths, or stories.
8	B	Ask relevant questions, seek clarification, and locate facts and details about stories and other texts and support answers with evidence from text.
9	A	Identify and use antonyms, synonyms, homographs, and homophones.
10	D	Make inferences about text and use textual evidence to support understanding.

Mini-Test 4, Informational Text

Question	Answer	TEKS Standard
1	C	Identify and use antonyms, synonyms, homographs, and homophones.
2	A	Use context to determine the relevant meaning of unfamiliar words or distinguish among multiple meaning words and homographs.
3	B	Use text features (e.g., bold print, captions, key words, italics) to locate information and make and verify predictions about contents of text.
4	A	Summarize information in text, maintaining meaning and logical order.
5	B	Draw conclusions from the facts presented in text and support those assertions with textual evidence.
6	B	Identify the details or facts that support the main idea.
7	C	Identify the details or facts that support the main idea.
8	B	Identify explicit cause and effect relationships among ideas in texts.
9	B	Make inferences about text and use textual evidence to support understanding.
10	D	Identify and use antonyms, synonyms, homographs, and homophones.

Mini-Test 5, Literary Text

Question	Answer	TEKS Standard
1	C	Identify and use antonyms, synonyms, homographs, and homophones.
2	B	Use context to determine the relevant meaning of unfamiliar words or distinguish among multiple meaning words and homographs.
3	C	Ask relevant questions, seek clarification, and locate facts and details about stories and other texts and support answers with evidence from text.
4	C	Make inferences about text and use textual evidence to support understanding.
5	B	Paraphrase the themes and supporting details of fables, legends, myths, or stories.
6	A	Paraphrase the themes and supporting details of fables, legends, myths, or stories.
7	D	Summarize information in text, maintaining meaning and logical order.
8	B	Sequence and summarize the plot's main events and explain their influence on future events.
9	A	Make inferences about text and use textual evidence to support understanding.
10	D	Describe the interaction of characters including their relationships and the changes they undergo.

Mini-Test 6, Informational Text

Question	Answer	TEKS Standard
1	C	Use context to determine the relevant meaning of unfamiliar words or distinguish among multiple meaning words and homographs.
2	B	Identify the meaning of common prefixes (e.g., in-, dis-) and suffixes (e.g., -full,-less), and know how they change the meaning of roots.
3	A	Use text features (e.g., bold print, captions, key words, italics) to locate information and make and verify predictions about contents of text.
4	C	Summarize information in text, maintaining meaning and logical order.
5	D	Make inferences about text and use textual evidence to support understanding.
6	C	Summarize information in text, maintaining meaning and logical order.
7	D	Identify explicit cause and effect relationships among ideas in texts.
8	B	Use context to determine the relevant meaning of unfamiliar words or distinguish among multiple meaning words and homographs.
9	A	Use text features (e.g., bold print, captions, key words, italics) to locate information and make and verify predictions about contents of text.
10	B	Draw conclusions from the facts presented in text and support those assertions with textual evidence.

Section 2: Vocabulary Quizzes

Quiz 1: Use Context to Determine Word Meaning

Question	Answer	TEKS Standard
1	B	Use context to determine the relevant meaning of unfamiliar words or distinguish among multiple meaning words and homographs.
2	B	
3	D	
4	C	
5	D	
6	B	
7	A	
8	B	
9	B	

Quiz 2: Understand and Use Synonyms

Question	Answer	TEKS Standard
1	A	Identify and use antonyms, synonyms, homographs, and homophones.
2	D	
3	C	
4	B	
5	C	
6	B	
7	C	
8	B	

Quiz 3: Understand and Use Antonyms

Question	Answer	TEKS Standard
1	A	Identify and use antonyms, synonyms, homographs, and homophones.
2	B	
3	C	
4	B	
5	D	
6	B	
7	D	
8	A	

Quiz 4: Use Homographs and Homophones

Question	Answer	TEKS Standard
1	C	Identify and use antonyms, synonyms, homographs, and homophones.
2	D	
3	B	
4	C	
5	A	
6	A	

Quiz 5: Understand and Use Prefixes

Question	Answer	TEKS Standard
1	D	Identify the meaning of common prefixes (e.g., in-, dis-) and suffixes (e.g., -full,-less), and know how they change the meaning of roots.
2	C	
3	A	
4	D	
5	B	
6	A	
7	A	
8	A	

Quiz 6: Understand and Use Suffixes

Question	Answer	TEKS Standard
1	C	Identify the meaning of common prefixes (e.g., in-, dis-) and suffixes (e.g., -full,-less), and know how they change the meaning of roots.
2	A	
3	D	
4	C	
5	A	
6	A	
7	B	
8	A	

Section 3: STAAR Reading Practice Test 1

Practice Test 1, Session 1

Question	Answer	TEKS Standard
1	D	Identify the meaning of common prefixes (e.g., in-, dis-) and suffixes (e.g., -full,-less), and know how they change the meaning of roots.
2	C	Identify explicit cause and effect relationships among ideas in texts.
3	B	Summarize information in text, maintaining meaning and logical order.
4	A	Identify and use antonyms, synonyms, homographs, and homophones.
5	C	Use text features (e.g., bold print, captions, key words, italics) to locate information and make and verify predictions about contents of text.
6	B	Use text features (e.g., bold print, captions, key words, italics) to locate information and make and verify predictions about contents of text.
7	B	Locate and use specific information in graphic features of text.
8	C	Use context to determine the relevant meaning of unfamiliar words or distinguish among multiple meaning words and homographs.
9	B	Identify the details or facts that support the main idea.
10	B	Identify and use antonyms, synonyms, homographs, and homophones.
11	B	Make inferences about text and use textual evidence to support understanding.
12	A	Describe the characteristics of various forms of poetry and how they create imagery (e.g., narrative poetry, lyrical poetry, humorous poetry, free verse).
13	C	Identify language that creates a graphic visual experience and appeals to the senses.
14	B	Ask relevant questions, seek clarification, and locate facts and details about stories and other texts and support answers with evidence from text.
15	C	Identify language that creates a graphic visual experience and appeals to the senses.
16	C	Summarize information in text, maintaining meaning and logical order.
17	C	Make inferences about text and use textual evidence to support understanding.
18	A	Use context to determine the relevant meaning of unfamiliar words or distinguish among multiple meaning words and homographs.
19	A	Identify and use antonyms, synonyms, homographs, and homophones.
20	D	Identify explicit cause and effect relationships among ideas in texts.
21	D	Draw conclusions from the facts presented in text and support those assertions with textual evidence.
22	C	Make inferences about text and use textual evidence to support understanding.
23	A	Summarize information in text, maintaining meaning and logical order.
24	C	Use text features (e.g., bold print, captions, key words, italics) to locate information and make and verify predictions about contents of text.

Practice Test 1, Session 2

Question	Answer	TEKS Standard
25	C	Use context to determine the relevant meaning of unfamiliar words or distinguish among multiple meaning words and homographs.
26	D	Identify and use antonyms, synonyms, homographs, and homophones.
27	A	Ask relevant questions, seek clarification, and locate facts and details about stories and other texts and support answers with evidence from text.
28	B	Make inferences about text and use textual evidence to support understanding.
29	B	Sequence and summarize the plot's main events and explain their influence on future events.
30	B	Describe the interaction of characters including their relationships and the changes they undergo.
31	C	Sequence and summarize the plot's main events and explain their influence on future events.
32	D	Ask relevant questions, seek clarification, and locate facts and details about stories and other texts and support answers with evidence from text.
33	B	Make inferences about text and use textual evidence to support understanding.
34	C	Use context to determine the relevant meaning of unfamiliar words or distinguish among multiple meaning words and homographs.
35	C	Identify and use antonyms, synonyms, homographs, and homophones.
36	A	Draw conclusions from the facts presented in text and support those assertions with textual evidence.
37	B	Identify explicit cause and effect relationships among ideas in texts.
38	C	Use comprehension skills to analyze how words, images, graphics, and sounds work together in various forms to impact meaning.
39	D	Make inferences about text and use textual evidence to support understanding.
40	D	Summarize information in text, maintaining meaning and logical order.
41	A	Identify and use antonyms, synonyms, homographs, and homophones.
42	B	Identify and use antonyms, synonyms, homographs, and homophones.
43	B	Ask relevant questions, seek clarification, and locate facts and details about stories and other texts and support answers with evidence from text.
44	A	Use context to determine the relevant meaning of unfamiliar words or distinguish among multiple meaning words and homographs.
45	A	Summarize information in text, maintaining meaning and logical order.
46	A	Describe the interaction of characters including their relationships and the changes they undergo.
47	A	Sequence and summarize the plot's main events and explain their influence on future events.
48	D	Make inferences about text and use textual evidence to support understanding.

Section 4: STAAR Reading Practice Test 2

Practice Test 2, Session 1

Question	Answer	TEKS Standard
1	C	Identify the meaning of common prefixes (e.g., in-, dis-) and suffixes (e.g., -full,-less), and know how they change the meaning of roots.
2	B	Use context to determine the relevant meaning of unfamiliar words or distinguish among multiple meaning words and homographs.
3	C	Draw conclusions from the facts presented in text and support those assertions with textual evidence.
4	A	Summarize information in text, maintaining meaning and logical order.
5	D	Identify the details or facts that support the main idea.
6	A	Make inferences about text and use textual evidence to support understanding.
7	B	Summarize information in text, maintaining meaning and logical order.
8	C	Make inferences about text and use textual evidence to support understanding.
9	A	Use context to determine the relevant meaning of unfamiliar words or distinguish among multiple meaning words and homographs.
10	C	Identify and use antonyms, synonyms, homographs, and homophones.
11	D	Describe the interaction of characters including their relationships and the changes they undergo.
12	A	Make inferences about text and use textual evidence to support understanding.
13	C	Identify language that creates a graphic visual experience and appeals to the senses.
14	D	Ask relevant questions, seek clarification, and locate facts and details about stories and other texts and support answers with evidence from text.
15	A	Sequence and summarize the plot's main events and explain their influence on future events.
16	C	Paraphrase the themes and supporting details of fables, legends, myths, or stories.
17	B	Make inferences about text and use textual evidence to support understanding.
18	C	Identify the meaning of common prefixes (e.g., in-, dis-) and suffixes (e.g., -full,-less), and know how they change the meaning of roots.
19	A	Use text features (e.g., bold print, captions, key words, italics) to locate information and make and verify predictions about contents of text.
20	B	Summarize information in text, maintaining meaning and logical order.
21	B	Draw conclusions from the facts presented in text and support those assertions with textual evidence.
22	B	Identify and use antonyms, synonyms, homographs, and homophones.
23	A	Use text features (e.g., bold print, captions, key words, italics) to locate information and make and verify predictions about contents of text.
24	C	Identify the details or facts that support the main idea.

Practice Test 2, Session 2

Question	Answer	TEKS Standard
25	C	Ask relevant questions, seek clarification, and locate facts and details about stories and other texts and support answers with evidence from text.
26	A	Identify language that creates a graphic visual experience and appeals to the senses.
27	C	Describe the characteristics of various forms of poetry and how they create imagery (e.g., narrative poetry, lyrical poetry, humorous poetry, free verse).
28	C	Use comprehension skills to analyze how words, images, graphics, and sounds work together in various forms to impact meaning.
29	D	Use context to determine the relevant meaning of unfamiliar words or distinguish among multiple meaning words and homographs.
30	D	Make inferences about text and use textual evidence to support understanding.
31	A	Use comprehension skills to analyze how words, images, graphics, and sounds work together in various forms to impact meaning.
32	B	Identify and use antonyms, synonyms, homographs, and homophones.
33	B	Identify and use antonyms, synonyms, homographs, and homophones.
34	B	Make inferences about text and use textual evidence to support understanding.
35	A	Summarize information in text, maintaining meaning and logical order.
36	C	Use context to determine the relevant meaning of unfamiliar words or distinguish among multiple meaning words and homographs.
37	A	Draw conclusions from the facts presented in text and support those assertions with textual evidence.
38	D	Use text features (e.g., bold print, captions, key words, italics) to locate information and make and verify predictions about contents of text.
39	B	Locate and use specific information in graphic features of text.
40	A	Summarize information in text, maintaining meaning and logical order.
41	B	Identify language that creates a graphic visual experience and appeals to the senses.
42	C	Ask relevant questions, seek clarification, and locate facts and details about stories and other texts and support answers with evidence from text.
43	B	Understand, make inferences and draw conclusions about the varied structural patterns and features of literary nonfiction and respond by providing evidence from text to support their understanding.
44	A	Describe the interaction of characters including their relationships and the changes they undergo.
45	B	Make inferences about text and use textual evidence to support understanding.
46	D	Describe the interaction of characters including their relationships and the changes they undergo.
47	B	Sequence and summarize the plot's main events and explain their influence on future events.
48	C	Use comprehension skills to analyze how words, images, graphics, and sounds work together in various forms to impact meaning.

Section 1: Reading Mini-Tests

	Mini-Test 1		Mini-Test 2		Mini-Test 3
1	Ⓐ Ⓑ Ⓒ Ⓓ	1	Ⓐ Ⓑ Ⓒ Ⓓ	1	Ⓐ Ⓑ Ⓒ Ⓓ
2	Ⓐ Ⓑ Ⓒ Ⓓ	2	Ⓐ Ⓑ Ⓒ Ⓓ	2	Ⓐ Ⓑ Ⓒ Ⓓ
3	Ⓐ Ⓑ Ⓒ Ⓓ	3	Ⓐ Ⓑ Ⓒ Ⓓ	3	Ⓐ Ⓑ Ⓒ Ⓓ
4	Ⓐ Ⓑ Ⓒ Ⓓ	4	Ⓐ Ⓑ Ⓒ Ⓓ	4	Ⓐ Ⓑ Ⓒ Ⓓ
5	Ⓐ Ⓑ Ⓒ Ⓓ	5	Ⓐ Ⓑ Ⓒ Ⓓ	5	Ⓐ Ⓑ Ⓒ Ⓓ
6	Ⓐ Ⓑ Ⓒ Ⓓ	6	Ⓐ Ⓑ Ⓒ Ⓓ	6	Ⓐ Ⓑ Ⓒ Ⓓ
7	Ⓐ Ⓑ Ⓒ Ⓓ	7	Ⓐ Ⓑ Ⓒ Ⓓ	7	Ⓐ Ⓑ Ⓒ Ⓓ
8	Ⓐ Ⓑ Ⓒ Ⓓ	8	Ⓐ Ⓑ Ⓒ Ⓓ	8	Ⓐ Ⓑ Ⓒ Ⓓ
9	Ⓐ Ⓑ Ⓒ Ⓓ	9	Ⓐ Ⓑ Ⓒ Ⓓ	9	Ⓐ Ⓑ Ⓒ Ⓓ
10	Ⓐ Ⓑ Ⓒ Ⓓ	10	Ⓐ Ⓑ Ⓒ Ⓓ	10	Ⓐ Ⓑ Ⓒ Ⓓ

	Mini-Test 4		Mini-Test 5		Mini-Test 6
1	Ⓐ Ⓑ Ⓒ Ⓓ	1	Ⓐ Ⓑ Ⓒ Ⓓ	1	Ⓐ Ⓑ Ⓒ Ⓓ
2	Ⓐ Ⓑ Ⓒ Ⓓ	2	Ⓐ Ⓑ Ⓒ Ⓓ	2	Ⓐ Ⓑ Ⓒ Ⓓ
3	Ⓐ Ⓑ Ⓒ Ⓓ	3	Ⓐ Ⓑ Ⓒ Ⓓ	3	Ⓐ Ⓑ Ⓒ Ⓓ
4	Ⓐ Ⓑ Ⓒ Ⓓ	4	Ⓐ Ⓑ Ⓒ Ⓓ	4	Ⓐ Ⓑ Ⓒ Ⓓ
5	Ⓐ Ⓑ Ⓒ Ⓓ	5	Ⓐ Ⓑ Ⓒ Ⓓ	5	Ⓐ Ⓑ Ⓒ Ⓓ
6	Ⓐ Ⓑ Ⓒ Ⓓ	6	Ⓐ Ⓑ Ⓒ Ⓓ	6	Ⓐ Ⓑ Ⓒ Ⓓ
7	Ⓐ Ⓑ Ⓒ Ⓓ	7	Ⓐ Ⓑ Ⓒ Ⓓ	7	Ⓐ Ⓑ Ⓒ Ⓓ
8	Ⓐ Ⓑ Ⓒ Ⓓ	8	Ⓐ Ⓑ Ⓒ Ⓓ	8	Ⓐ Ⓑ Ⓒ Ⓓ
9	Ⓐ Ⓑ Ⓒ Ⓓ	9	Ⓐ Ⓑ Ⓒ Ⓓ	9	Ⓐ Ⓑ Ⓒ Ⓓ
10	Ⓐ Ⓑ Ⓒ Ⓓ	10	Ⓐ Ⓑ Ⓒ Ⓓ	10	Ⓐ Ⓑ Ⓒ Ⓓ

Section 2: Vocabulary Quizzes

	Quiz 1		Quiz 2		Quiz 3
1	Ⓐ Ⓑ Ⓒ Ⓓ	1	Ⓐ Ⓑ Ⓒ Ⓓ	1	Ⓐ Ⓑ Ⓒ Ⓓ
2	Ⓐ Ⓑ Ⓒ Ⓓ	2	Ⓐ Ⓑ Ⓒ Ⓓ	2	Ⓐ Ⓑ Ⓒ Ⓓ
3	Ⓐ Ⓑ Ⓒ Ⓓ	3	Ⓐ Ⓑ Ⓒ Ⓓ	3	Ⓐ Ⓑ Ⓒ Ⓓ
4	Ⓐ Ⓑ Ⓒ Ⓓ	4	Ⓐ Ⓑ Ⓒ Ⓓ	4	Ⓐ Ⓑ Ⓒ Ⓓ
5	Ⓐ Ⓑ Ⓒ Ⓓ	5	Ⓐ Ⓑ Ⓒ Ⓓ	5	Ⓐ Ⓑ Ⓒ Ⓓ
6	Ⓐ Ⓑ Ⓒ Ⓓ	6	Ⓐ Ⓑ Ⓒ Ⓓ	6	Ⓐ Ⓑ Ⓒ Ⓓ
7	Ⓐ Ⓑ Ⓒ Ⓓ	7	Ⓐ Ⓑ Ⓒ Ⓓ	7	Ⓐ Ⓑ Ⓒ Ⓓ
8	Ⓐ Ⓑ Ⓒ Ⓓ	8	Ⓐ Ⓑ Ⓒ Ⓓ	8	Ⓐ Ⓑ Ⓒ Ⓓ
9	Ⓐ Ⓑ Ⓒ Ⓓ				

	Quiz 4		Quiz 5		Quiz 6
1	Ⓐ Ⓑ Ⓒ Ⓓ	1	Ⓐ Ⓑ Ⓒ Ⓓ	1	Ⓐ Ⓑ Ⓒ Ⓓ
2	Ⓐ Ⓑ Ⓒ Ⓓ	2	Ⓐ Ⓑ Ⓒ Ⓓ	2	Ⓐ Ⓑ Ⓒ Ⓓ
3	Ⓐ Ⓑ Ⓒ Ⓓ	3	Ⓐ Ⓑ Ⓒ Ⓓ	3	Ⓐ Ⓑ Ⓒ Ⓓ
4	Ⓐ Ⓑ Ⓒ Ⓓ	4	Ⓐ Ⓑ Ⓒ Ⓓ	4	Ⓐ Ⓑ Ⓒ Ⓓ
5	Ⓐ Ⓑ Ⓒ Ⓓ	5	Ⓐ Ⓑ Ⓒ Ⓓ	5	Ⓐ Ⓑ Ⓒ Ⓓ
6	Ⓐ Ⓑ Ⓒ Ⓓ	6	Ⓐ Ⓑ Ⓒ Ⓓ	6	Ⓐ Ⓑ Ⓒ Ⓓ
		7	Ⓐ Ⓑ Ⓒ Ⓓ	7	Ⓐ Ⓑ Ⓒ Ⓓ
		8	Ⓐ Ⓑ Ⓒ Ⓓ	8	Ⓐ Ⓑ Ⓒ Ⓓ

Section 3: STAAR Reading Practice Test 1

STAAR Reading Practice Test 1: Session 1

#		#		#	
1	Ⓐ Ⓑ Ⓒ Ⓓ	9	Ⓐ Ⓑ Ⓒ Ⓓ	17	Ⓐ Ⓑ Ⓒ Ⓓ
2	Ⓐ Ⓑ Ⓒ Ⓓ	10	Ⓐ Ⓑ Ⓒ Ⓓ	18	Ⓐ Ⓑ Ⓒ Ⓓ
3	Ⓐ Ⓑ Ⓒ Ⓓ	11	Ⓐ Ⓑ Ⓒ Ⓓ	19	Ⓐ Ⓑ Ⓒ Ⓓ
4	Ⓐ Ⓑ Ⓒ Ⓓ	12	Ⓐ Ⓑ Ⓒ Ⓓ	20	Ⓐ Ⓑ Ⓒ Ⓓ
5	Ⓐ Ⓑ Ⓒ Ⓓ	13	Ⓐ Ⓑ Ⓒ Ⓓ	21	Ⓐ Ⓑ Ⓒ Ⓓ
6	Ⓐ Ⓑ Ⓒ Ⓓ	14	Ⓐ Ⓑ Ⓒ Ⓓ	22	Ⓐ Ⓑ Ⓒ Ⓓ
7	Ⓐ Ⓑ Ⓒ Ⓓ	15	Ⓐ Ⓑ Ⓒ Ⓓ	23	Ⓐ Ⓑ Ⓒ Ⓓ
8	Ⓐ Ⓑ Ⓒ Ⓓ	16	Ⓐ Ⓑ Ⓒ Ⓓ	24	Ⓐ Ⓑ Ⓒ Ⓓ

STAAR Reading Practice Test 1: Session 2

#		#		#	
25	Ⓐ Ⓑ Ⓒ Ⓓ	33	Ⓐ Ⓑ Ⓒ Ⓓ	41	Ⓐ Ⓑ Ⓒ Ⓓ
26	Ⓐ Ⓑ Ⓒ Ⓓ	34	Ⓐ Ⓑ Ⓒ Ⓓ	42	Ⓐ Ⓑ Ⓒ Ⓓ
27	Ⓐ Ⓑ Ⓒ Ⓓ	35	Ⓐ Ⓑ Ⓒ Ⓓ	43	Ⓐ Ⓑ Ⓒ Ⓓ
28	Ⓐ Ⓑ Ⓒ Ⓓ	36	Ⓐ Ⓑ Ⓒ Ⓓ	44	Ⓐ Ⓑ Ⓒ Ⓓ
29	Ⓐ Ⓑ Ⓒ Ⓓ	37	Ⓐ Ⓑ Ⓒ Ⓓ	45	Ⓐ Ⓑ Ⓒ Ⓓ
30	Ⓐ Ⓑ Ⓒ Ⓓ	38	Ⓐ Ⓑ Ⓒ Ⓓ	46	Ⓐ Ⓑ Ⓒ Ⓓ
31	Ⓐ Ⓑ Ⓒ Ⓓ	39	Ⓐ Ⓑ Ⓒ Ⓓ	47	Ⓐ Ⓑ Ⓒ Ⓓ
32	Ⓐ Ⓑ Ⓒ Ⓓ	40	Ⓐ Ⓑ Ⓒ Ⓓ	48	Ⓐ Ⓑ Ⓒ Ⓓ

Section 4: STAAR Reading Practice Test 2

STAAR Reading Practice Test 2: Session 1

#		#		#	
1	Ⓐ Ⓑ Ⓒ Ⓓ	9	Ⓐ Ⓑ Ⓒ Ⓓ	17	Ⓐ Ⓑ Ⓒ Ⓓ
2	Ⓐ Ⓑ Ⓒ Ⓓ	10	Ⓐ Ⓑ Ⓒ Ⓓ	18	Ⓐ Ⓑ Ⓒ Ⓓ
3	Ⓐ Ⓑ Ⓒ Ⓓ	11	Ⓐ Ⓑ Ⓒ Ⓓ	19	Ⓐ Ⓑ Ⓒ Ⓓ
4	Ⓐ Ⓑ Ⓒ Ⓓ	12	Ⓐ Ⓑ Ⓒ Ⓓ	20	Ⓐ Ⓑ Ⓒ Ⓓ
5	Ⓐ Ⓑ Ⓒ Ⓓ	13	Ⓐ Ⓑ Ⓒ Ⓓ	21	Ⓐ Ⓑ Ⓒ Ⓓ
6	Ⓐ Ⓑ Ⓒ Ⓓ	14	Ⓐ Ⓑ Ⓒ Ⓓ	22	Ⓐ Ⓑ Ⓒ Ⓓ
7	Ⓐ Ⓑ Ⓒ Ⓓ	15	Ⓐ Ⓑ Ⓒ Ⓓ	23	Ⓐ Ⓑ Ⓒ Ⓓ
8	Ⓐ Ⓑ Ⓒ Ⓓ	16	Ⓐ Ⓑ Ⓒ Ⓓ	24	Ⓐ Ⓑ Ⓒ Ⓓ

STAAR Reading Practice Test 2: Session 2

#		#		#	
25	Ⓐ Ⓑ Ⓒ Ⓓ	33	Ⓐ Ⓑ Ⓒ Ⓓ	41	Ⓐ Ⓑ Ⓒ Ⓓ
26	Ⓐ Ⓑ Ⓒ Ⓓ	34	Ⓐ Ⓑ Ⓒ Ⓓ	42	Ⓐ Ⓑ Ⓒ Ⓓ
27	Ⓐ Ⓑ Ⓒ Ⓓ	35	Ⓐ Ⓑ Ⓒ Ⓓ	43	Ⓐ Ⓑ Ⓒ Ⓓ
28	Ⓐ Ⓑ Ⓒ Ⓓ	36	Ⓐ Ⓑ Ⓒ Ⓓ	44	Ⓐ Ⓑ Ⓒ Ⓓ
29	Ⓐ Ⓑ Ⓒ Ⓓ	37	Ⓐ Ⓑ Ⓒ Ⓓ	45	Ⓐ Ⓑ Ⓒ Ⓓ
30	Ⓐ Ⓑ Ⓒ Ⓓ	38	Ⓐ Ⓑ Ⓒ Ⓓ	46	Ⓐ Ⓑ Ⓒ Ⓓ
31	Ⓐ Ⓑ Ⓒ Ⓓ	39	Ⓐ Ⓑ Ⓒ Ⓓ	47	Ⓐ Ⓑ Ⓒ Ⓓ
32	Ⓐ Ⓑ Ⓒ Ⓓ	40	Ⓐ Ⓑ Ⓒ Ⓓ	48	Ⓐ Ⓑ Ⓒ Ⓓ

Made in the USA
Lexington, KY
08 January 2016